The Child and Society

Studies in Sociology

Consulting Editor: Charles H. Page

University of Massachusetts

Frederick Elkin
York University, Toronto

Gerald Handel
The City College of the City University
of New York

The Child and Society:
The Process of Socialization

Second Edition

 Random House · New York

ISBN: 0-394-31192-2

Library of Congress Catalog Card Number: 79-169696

Manufactured in the United States of America.
Composed by Cherry Hill Composition, Pennsauken, N.J.
Printed and bound by Halliday Lithograph Corp.,
West Hanover, Mass.

Second Edition
9 8 7 6 5 4 3 2 1

Typography by Andrea Clark
Cover design by Wendell Minor

Dedicated to **Madge**
F. E.

and to
Ruth, Jonathan, and Michael
G. H.

Preface

Since the first edition of this book was published in 1960 there has been an enormous amount of research and thought about socialization, clearly necessitating an updating and rethinking of this book. The new material in anthropology, human development, political science, psychiatry, psychology, sociology, and other disciplines concerned with socialization is far too voluminous and diverse to be absorbed into a brief introductory treatment. We have had to be selective. The goal of this revision is unchanged from that of the first edition: to provide a coherent treatment, from a sociological standpoint, of how children are socialized into modern society.

Many diverse disciplines have felt the need for a sociologically focused treatment of socialization. We are pleased that the first edition has so often filled this need in sociology, psychology, child development, education, social work, child psychiatry, pediatric nursing, and other fields in which an understanding of children and society is sought. We hope that this fresh look will prove similarly helpful.

Chapters 1 and 2 have been amplified and altered, but in relatively minor ways. Chapter 3, "The Processes of Socialization," is virtually entirely new. Chapters 4 and 5 have been substantially rewritten and enlarged, and their order has been reversed. Chapter 6, a coda to the first edition, has here been expanded to bring out more fully—if still only schematically—the relationship between childhood and subsequent socialization.

The basic plan of the book is unchanged from the first edition, of which Frederick Elkin was sole author. Responsibility for drafting this revision was assumed by Gerald Handel. Final review of the manuscript was the collaborative effort of both authors.

Thanks are expressed to Betty Yorburg for comments on the first draft of Chapters 1, 2, and 3 and to Fred Davis for comments on the first draft of Chapter 6. Our appreciation is expressed also to Mrs. Vivian Cox, who typed the first draft of the manuscript, and to Mrs. Teresa Trott, who typed the second. Regarding both editions, we thank Charles H. Page for his encouragement and extremely helpful suggestions on style and content.

Frederick Elkin
Gerald Handel

Contents

The Child and Society

1 Socialization Defined

As a child grows, he develops in many ways. Physically he becomes taller, heavier, stronger, and capable of such activities as walking, talking, writing, riding a bicycle, and, later, having sexual relations. Mentally, he becomes capable of such activities as memorizing poems, working out problems in algebra, imagining love scenes, and acquiring the knowledge necessary to carry through a job. He also develops a more or less consistent personality structure, so that he can be characterized, for example, as shy, modest, bold, persistent, frugal, or friendly. However, such lines of development in themselves are of limited value in explaining how someone functions in the society. They do not tell us, for example, what behavior to expect from a doctor or a department store clerk, what hardware stores or hospitals are for, what utensils to use when eating specific foods, how to behave in church, or what to do if giving a party. Nor do they touch on the feelings an individual develops toward his sister, his music teacher, his peer group, his country. Nor do they indicate the standards of right and wrong he upholds or his feelings if he is inadvertently rude, fails an examination, considers taking drugs, or in some other way does not measure up to his own expectations or the expectations of others.

The baby, of course, knows nothing of these ways of his society; but he has the potentialities to learn them. His potentialities are in fact wide and varied. In one setting he will speak English, in another, Russian; in one he will eat rice with chopsticks, in another, with a fork; in one he will stand and feel proud if "La Marseillaise" is played, in another the music would have to be "God Save the Queen"; in one he will be deeply respectful to his father, in another he will speak to him as a "pal"; in one he will feel somber and serious at a funeral, in another he will feel and express strong emotion; in one he will eat grasshoppers with zest, in another he will turn away in disgust.

It is with such questions that the socialization of the child is concerned. We may define socialization as *the process by which someone learns the ways of a given society or social group so that he can function within it.* As the examples above illustrate, many kinds of learning are encompassed within this general process. Some of what is learned is overt and visible, such as using the proper eating utensil or wearing appropriate clothes for different kinds of occasions. But even these overt behaviors can be understood only if we recognize that they come to be guided by more generalized learning whose effects are not directly visible but must be inferred. Put otherwise, the child learns to be concerned with appropriateness as a general guide to his conduct. He develops a "sense of propriety," which not only governs his behavior in situations comparable to those he has already experienced but which also guides him in dealing with new situations that he encounters for the first time. Thus, when he enters a new group, he does so with some sense of how to act, because he has learned to be concerned with acting appropriately in a group. When he takes his first job, he is not at a total loss, because he has had experience in other situations that have the quality of "being supervised by someone with authority to supervise." Of course, the person then goes on to learn the specific requirements for membership in his new group or the requirements for being supervised as an employee, which are different from the kind of supervision he received as a child from his parents or as a pupil from his teachers.

In addition to learning specific overt behaviors and a general sense of appropriateness, the child also learns to experience certain specific emotions in specific kinds of situations. He may learn to feel possessive with property, or he may learn to feel indifferent to it. He may learn to feel proud at winning a fist fight or ashamed for having gotten into one.

Some of what the child learns in the course of being socialized is explicitly taught by people who have the obligation to teach him, as when he learns to use eating utensils or to feel patriotic. Parents and teachers are specifically entrusted by society with the task of preparing the young to become qualified participants in society. But some of the learning that is included in socialization is self-motivated, and the child develops and builds on a constantly changing base. Having first become responsive to his parents, he has been prepared to be responsive to others. Early on, the child begins to see in other people models for what he might like to become, and at home he is apt to take his parents as models for behavior in which they do not instruct him. If father brings home a briefcase, his five-year-old son may pick it up and carry it around "like Daddy." Policemen and firemen are early heroes of many young children, and the child sees them, at least for a time, as models for his own later behavior.

Socialization is, then, a process that helps explain two different kinds of phenomena. On the one hand, it helps to explain how a person becomes capable of participating in society. For it is clear that the newborn infant is not a social being. Most of the qualities we regard as human are present in the child only as potentialities. In the early days of his life, the infant experiences hunger pangs, cries, gains relaxation of his tension by sucking on a source of nourishment, experiences visceral tension, and gains relaxation by excretion. In short, the newborn's capacities for functioning with other human beings are exceedingly minimal. They are developed through socialization.

On the other hand, socialization helps to explain how society is possible at all. While certain species of animals lower in the evolutionary scale function in rudimentary societies, none of these approaches the complexity of human society, which takes so many different forms and is elaborated with infinite subtleties. Consequently, looking at man from the perspective of evolution, it is necessary to explain how vast numbers of organisms called human are able to attune their actions to one another in such a way as to make possible an ongoing social order. While a full explanation, insofar as one is possible, would take us far beyond the subject matter of this book, the socialization process is one key element of such an explanation. Social order is possible because the human infant encounters adults who teach him and from whom he can learn to regulate his actions in accord with various standards of appropriateness.

As implied in some of our earlier examples, the process of socialization is not confined to infancy and childhood. It is now recognized that socialization continues throughout the life cycle of the individual. The term socialization refers to learning the ways of any established and continuing group: An immigrant becomes socialized into the life of his new country, a recruit into the life of the Army, and a new insurance agent into the patterns of his company and his job. The recognition of the continuing nature of socialization has led to the recent concept of *adult socialization*. The term takes account of the fact that adults are obliged to go through certain experiences and developments somewhat similar to those undergone by infants and children, although there is a basic difference in that later socialization is built upon an already acquired capacity to evaluate one's own behavior and function as a social being.

Having thus delineated the basic nature of socialization, it will be useful to indicate some problems that are not encompassed by this concept. First, it is not a problem of socialization to explain or speculate upon how a society or social group began. The society into which the child is born, with its common expectations, ways of doing things, standards of right and wrong, and current trends, is the result of a unique historical evolution and exists before the child enters it. Socialization begins with the assumption of this ongoing preexisting society.

Second, socialization is not concerned with the impact of new members on the society or on given groups. Socialization is not strictly a one-way process. The entrance of a new member into a family, or into any unit, changes the group. It is not just the old group with one added person; it is a *new* group with new relationships and a new organization. But only insofar as the interrelationships affect the socialization process is this new reorganization directly relevant to our interests in this book.

Third, socialization does not try to explain the uniqueness of individuals. Although it is true that no two individuals are alike and that each person has a singular heredity, distinctive experiences, and a unique personality development, socialization focuses not on such individualizing patterns and processes, but on similarities, on aspects of development that concern the learning of and adaptation to the culture and society. In the course of development the child goes through two major developmental processes simultaneously: individuation and socialization. In his earliest years the child does not experience this distinction, but at later ages he does become capable of recognizing such a distinction in his life experience. He is able to do so, however, only if he has been socialized in a way that permits the kind of individuation that allows him to perceive distinctions of this kind.

This study deals with the process of socialization, with the problem of how the child becomes a functioning member of the society. We shall use a wide range of illustrations, but generally they will come from North American society and from the middle-class groups with which we are most familiar. However, we shall also give some attention to socialization patterns that differ from the most familiar, as well as to socialization in later life. Chapter 2 discusses the basic preconditions for socialization and is followed by a consideration in Chapter 3 of the processes, mechanisms, and techniques by which it occurs. Chapter 4 considers socialization patterns of certain basic subdivisions in our society: social class, ethnic group, and community. Chapter 5 is concerned with the primary socializing agencies in our society: family, school, peer group, and media of mass communication. Socialization is intimately related to family life, and although the family is treated as such only in Chapter 5, ramifications of this relationship are discussed at various points throughout the book. The final chapter discusses later socialization and its relation to childhood.

2 Preconditions for Socialization

For a child to become adequately socialized, three preconditions are necessary. First, there must be *an ongoing society,* the world into which he is to be socialized. Second, the child must have the *requisite biological inheritance.* If he is feeble-minded or suffers from a serious organic mental disorder, adequate socialization will be impossible. Certain other biological deficits do not make socialization impossible but cause it to be beset by serious difficulties. Children born blind, deaf, or mute encounter special obstacles and are necessarily excluded from certain kinds of opportunities available to others. Nevertheless, such children—and those with such other disabilities as the malformed arms and legs suffered in recent years by children of mothers who took the drug thalidomide during pregnancy—can, with special training, achieve levels of socialization that permit them to function more or less satisfactorily in the society.

Third, a child requires *human nature.* This concept is not readily given a compact definition, but some of its fundamental components can be specified. Of particular significance is the ability to establish emotional relationships with others and to experience such sentiments as love, sympathy, shame, envy, pity, and pride. Scarcely less important is the ability to transform experience into symbols, which make possible speech, writing, and thought. Although writing is not, of course, necessary for adequate socialization—some societies have no writing at all, and in earlier periods of our own history a person could be adequately socialized without being able to read, let alone write—human socialization is not possible without speech; and speech depends upon the capacity to symbolize.

Each of these necessary preconditions is significant insofar as it points up basic background material for an understanding of socialization.

An Ongoing Society

A child is born into a world that already exists. He is a "raw recruit" into the world, an involuntary recruit, with no wish to be there and no knowledge of how to get along in it. From the point of view of society, the function of socialization is to transmit to new members the culture and motivation to participate in established social relationships. The society has a patterned consistency, so that one can predict, *within limits,* how people will behave, think, and feel. We may view this society from several perspectives, each of which points up certain distinctive features.

First, there is the perspective of *norms* and *values.* A norm is an implicit rule defining the appropriate pattern of behavior in a recurring situation. "Being clothed" is the norm when presenting oneself in a public place. This example indicates that a norm is both a standard by which behavior is judged and also a prediction as to what behavior is likely to occur. People are supposed to be clothed in public, and one may predict that in any public place the people one encounters will probably be clothed. Such convergence of the two meanings of "expected" (what should happen and what is predicted to happen) is never fully realized. Students are expected to study throughout the term—that is, they should do so. But it is also expected that some will do no more than cram before an examination—that is, one may predict that this is how they will study. The two meanings of expectation are not always carefully distinguished, and for many purposes it is sufficient to make the rough assumption that what should be done is what is generally done. Many social problems, however, arise from divergence of what happens from what is supposed to happen, and it is then necessary to distinguish ideal norms from behavioral norms.

Values are more general than norms. They are best thought of as conceptions of the desirable that serve as criteria for norms. A society in which freedom, for example, is a salient value will *tend* to develop norms consistent with that value in its economic practices, its educational methods, the relations between the sexes, the way it rears its children, and in other areas of life. This is not to say that all the norms in these situations are entirely consistent with freedom, for they are not. Other values tend to generate norms inconsistent with those of freedom, so that the norms governing any situation are not simple derivatives from a single value.

A second perspective is that of *status* and *role.* A status is a position in the social structure, and a role is the expected behavior of someone who holds a given status. We can cooperate with others because we know the rights and obligations associated with each status. The taxi driver has the right to ask you for your fare and the obligation to drive you to your destination; the physician has the right to ask about your symptoms and, in some instances, to ask you to remove your clothes; and he has the obligation to try to cure you. Similarly, role behavior is expected of the teacher, student, mother, father, daughter, grocery clerk, Roman Catholic, taxicab passenger, and doctor's patient. Each person has many statuses that define his expected behavior in given situations.

A third perspective is that of *institutions*, each of which focuses about a segment of life and consists of many norms and statuses. One such institution is the school, whose primary function is to transmit, in a more or less formal way, a large share of the intellectual heritage of a society. Within the school there are norms relating to attendance, sports events, courses, and holiday celebrations; and there are patterned status relationships among the teachers, students, principal, and custodians. The church, hospital, stock market, and congressional system are other institutions that are the foci for the organization of many activities. Despite a regular turnover of personnel these institutions continue to operate over a period of many years, in great part because each new generation is socialized into the appropriate patterns.

A fourth perspective focuses on cultural and group subdivisions within the larger society. One major subdivision is *social class*. Individuals in our society vary in the amounts of wealth, prestige, and power they possess; and associated with these variations are differences in values and ways of life. Social-class rankings may partake of all of these elements. At one extreme may be the upper-class individual who is wealthy, has an important business position, lives in a luxurious home, sends his children to private schools, and vacations in Europe. At the other extreme may be the lower-class individual who works as an unskilled laborer, left school at the age of fourteen, lives in a slum area, and has "crude" table manners. Between these extremes there are other rough rankings, from the professional man and lesser business executive to the white-collar worker to the skilled laborer. It is evident that no single characteristic clearly differentiates class groups, that the lines between them are blurred, and that there is interclass movement. But a stratification system of a kind does exist.

Another major subdivision in our society, one which over-laps considerably with social class, is the *ethnic group.* The population of North America has been built up of immigrants from many countries. In coming here they have kept some of their old-country characteristics, and they may be thought of as "different," both by others and by themselves. Thus, we find Italians, Greeks, Jews, Mexicans, Chinese, and French Canadians, who are distinguished from others by their names, language, traditional foods, holiday rituals, occupations, folk-lore, patterns of child rearing, and loyalties. A related division is the *racial minority*, which is also likely to be thought of as "different" both by others and by themselves. The most prom-inent racial minority in our society is the Negro, or black, as many now prefer to be identified.

Still another perspective is that of *social change*, especially important today because of the rapidity with which it occurs. The society into which a child is born is not static; there are conflicting pressures, a diffusion of materials and ideas, and general trends that shift direction. New technology, new experiences, and new decisions reverberate in many direc-tions, generating changes in values, norms, institutions, sta-tuses, roles, and intergroup relationships. The reader will readily identify some of the familiar changes that have been under way for some time: the movement of families to the suburbs; the increasing emancipation of women; the de-velopment of new careers in new industries; the tendency to professionalization of teachers, morticians, social workers, insurance agents, pharmacists, and other groups. Among the most dramatic have been the recent upsurges of student activism and black militancy. In these, as in the other changes, socialization, inasmuch as it involves a receptivity to modi-fication as well as given patterns of thought, feeling, and behavior, has a part to play.

There is, then, a complex and variable world, which may be approached from many perspectives, into which the child is to be socialized. In order to function within it, whether it be primarily as conformist or rebel, he must have at least a minimum of knowledge about this world and a minimum of what the culture defines as appropriate behavior and feelings. He must know what to expect from people of given statuses, how he himself fits in with the various groupings, what is considered proper and improper in given situations, and the range of alternative behavior possible in those segments of social life that are rapidly changing. This is the world that the socializers, knowingly or unknowingly, pass on to the newcomer.

Biological Inheritance

A second precondition for socialization is an adequate biological inheritance, or original nature. It is apparent that those who have certain serious hereditary deficiencies either cannot be socialized or will have distinctive problems in the process. Socialization depends, for example, upon memory. An adequate memory can develop only if the parts of the brain governing memory are sufficiently intact. A child born with serious injury to that area of the brain may be unable to develop the necessary level of memory. Thus, certain serious deficits in the biological organism preclude adequate socialization. Other organic deficiencies create problems but may be somewhat less fateful. A child born deaf will not learn to speak in the same way other children learn, since he cannot hear his own voice; but with special intensive training he can learn to speak. It is worth noting at this point that the extent to which biological deficit precludes adequate socialization does not depend entirely on the defect itself but on society's response to it as well. The deaf can be more adequately socialized today than formerly because our institutions chose to discover (with some success) ways of modifying deafness and its consequences. Intensified efforts have also been initiated in recent years to find ways to modify the deficit imposed by biologically induced mental retardation, so that this condition, too, may yield to the power of social organization. New norms and new institutions for coping with biological deficit yield new outcomes in socialization.

Although abnormal biological conditions present special problems in socialization, problems that may be recast by social advances, socialization is also intimately involved with biology for the organically normal individual. Certain biological characteristics set the context for socialization. First, the human organism is *helpless* and completely dependent at birth. It cannot survive without the intervention of persons who give it care. Now it is evident that physical survival depends upon the provision of nourishment and protection against temperature extremes; but there is also evidence, to be cited shortly, that these necessary rudiments of care may not be sufficient for the infant's survival, let alone for his adequate socialization. Responsiveness from other people appears to be necessary for survival itself.

The newborns of many species are helpless and dependent at birth, but the human offspring has the *most prolonged dependency* of any. Lower forms of life—animals, birds, and insects—can often function well merely by following inborn instincts. The bird knows how to build its nest, the bee knows what foods to eat and what particular job it has in the colony, and the lion knows how to hunt and how to protect its young. These are inborn patterns of goal-directed activity that have persisted relatively unchanged for thousands of years. No comparable built-in mechanisms exist in human beings, and in order to function within society, we must learn from others how to build homes, earn a living, and take care of our children.

A third basic biological fact is *maturation.* The human organism develops according to a fairly set timetable, which varies within rather narrow limits. This timetable helps to shape the course of socialization. The newborn infant cannot immediately be trained to use eating utensils, whether these be chopsticks or knife and fork; a minimum level of eye-hand coordination must be achieved first. And, although a six-months-old infant may be "possessive" of his rattle, the social importance of "respect for property" can be communicated only when neuromuscular development allows walking and permits the toddler to reach for fragile lamps and other breakables.

The evolutionary development of certain specific organs is particularly important as a foundation for socialization. The development of the outermost layer of the human brain—the cortex—is a prerequisite to socialization. Vocal organs capable of highly varied speech (rather than merely a few grunts or tweets); the fact of being two-footed rather than four-footed; the fact that sexual drives are not restricted, as in many other animals, to a periodic mating season—these are some of the organismic characteristics of the human that serve as determinants of or (looked at in another way) resources for socialization.

Although the biological character of the organism and the timetable of maturation set certain outer limits to human variation, a no less significant factor is the psychobiological *plasticity* of the human body. Thus, a child inherits certain "mass movements," impulses that are expressed in random undefined directions. For example, he makes numerous different sounds and moves his fingers in a variety of ways. Whether these sounds are eventually organized into the English, Spanish, or Chinese language, or whether the finger movements come to include the ability to write, manipulate utensils, or play musical instruments, are functions of the specific definitions and guidance given by people in the surrounding world. Drives such as hunger, thirst, sleep, and sex can be satisfied in many ways. The need for food may be satisfied by eating meat, vegetables, insects, or even people. Sex needs may be expressed directly or sublimated in dancing, art, or religious ceremonies; they may be directed toward people within or outside certain groups; they may be suppressed before marriage or encouraged and directed to certain specific outlets. Which foods or which forms of sex expression are preferred will reflect social and psychological influences. Such influences can be meaningful only because the body allows variation.

Not to be overlooked are other types of variation. A child is born with certain temperamental tendencies toward passivity or activity, perhaps toward restlessness; and he is also born with certain sensitivities. Such tendencies are evidenced from birth in a baby's movements, sleeping and crying habits, frustration tolerance, and responses to food. These temperamental tendencies gain some of their significance from the interpretations of those who react to them. An "active" baby will receive one kind of response if his parents enjoy an active baby and quite another response if they would be more comfortable with a placid and docile child.

Similarly, the development of intelligence and particular talents cannot be separated from the surrounding world. Indeed, in no aspect of human development is it more futile to ask what proportion derives from original nature and what proportion from experience. Since *all* intelligence is "experienced" intelligence—that is, an indeterminate blend of native potentiality and experience—there is no known way to measure "native intelligence." Whether a particular potentiality is actually developed and what direction development takes depend upon the possibilities that are available, the encouragement that comes from others, and the growth of the personality structure. A society without paints would not know Picasso, and neither Mozart nor baseball star Mickey Mantle would have become what they did in Mozambique. Neither would they have succeeded if their personalities were so disturbed that they could not focus their attention long enough to develop their talents and abilities.

Clearly then the biological nature of man—the form and transformation of the body through time—both allows and requires socialization; and certain biological requisites are necessary for an adequate socialization. For purposes of analysis it is necessary to identify the biological substratum underlying socialization, but in actual situations biological factors become so closely interlinked with elements of the social world that it is often impossible to isolate empirically the hereditary from the environmental and to weight the importance of each.

Human Nature

A third precondition for socialization is what Charles H. Cooley, the early American sociologist, called human nature. What he wished to emphasize by this term is something distinctive to humans as compared to other animals and yet something universal among humans, not a product of only some societies. According to Cooley, a fully developed human nature is a product rather than a precondition of socialization. Yet the infant must have certain prototypical capacities out of which his full human nature can develop. In the following discussion we shall briefly delineate Cooley's concept of human nature and then specify the capacities that underlie it.

To Cooley, human nature consists of sentiments. He regards sympathy as the most basic sentiment, one which enters into such other sentiments as love, resentment, ambition, vanity, hero worship, and the "feeling of social right and wrong." He writes:

Human nature in this sense is justly regarded as a comparatively permanent element in society. Always and everywhere men seek honor and dread ridicule, defer to public opinion, cherish their goods and their children, and admire courage, generosity, and success. It is always safe to assume that people are and have been human.[1]

From our present perspective, more than sixty years after Cooley and with much intervening experience and research, we know that the situation is more complex than he described it. Some men will brave ridicule rather than dread it; not all defer to public opinion, nor do all cherish their children. But certain of his fundamental observations are durable: Such sentiments as honor and ridicule, courage and generosity are distinctively human and possible in all human societies and thus are not limited to certain cultures, although they receive varying emphasis and are expressed differently in different cultures.

Such complex sentiments as pride, embarrassment, cruelty, and envy are based on two human capacities. One is *the ability to empathize* with others, to place oneself imaginatively in their positions and to be aware of their feelings. Although the lower animals have the ability to form emotional attachments, they do not, as far as we know, have the capacity to empathize. We assume, for example, that a cat that toys with a mouse is unaware of the feelings of the mouse and therefore is not, in Cooley's sense, "cruel"; nor is a large dog that attacks a small one and takes his bone "unkind." However, a prison guard who tortures a prisoner or refuses him food is very much aware of the prisoner's suffering.

The second capacity on which such sentiments rest is *the ability to symbolize*—that is, to give meaning, both cognitively and emotionally, to sounds, gestures, and signs of various kinds. Man's symbolic capacities are often described as though they were only intellectual in nature. The capacity for intellectual symbolization is certainly important, but it is not the whole of symbolization by any means. We shall cite a few familiar examples.

If a person clenches and shakes his fist at someone, the recipient understands that the person is angry and wants him to feel threatened and afraid. The gesture is a symbol: It stands for something other than itself. It stands for a threat and feeling in the one who makes the gesture and for an anticipated response in the one who receives it.

As another example, the prison guard who inflicts torture

wishes to see the prisoner suffer; that is, he wishes to bring about certain responses which, when they occur, will give him satisfaction. This kind of satisfaction, unlike that of animal hunger or sex, can only be understood in terms of man's ability to symbolize. The prisoner's behavior—screaming or pleading or whatever—represents for the guard a symbolization of himself, perhaps as strong or tough or in authority. (Perhaps also the guard's state of mind, with its complex of meanings and gratifications, may be found in his fellow guards and be part of an institutional norm.) The prisoner, in turn, might refuse the guard his sought-for self-image by remaining stoic and expressing no pain.

Still another example: A teacher awards a student an "A" for a term paper—intending it to be a cognitive symbol representing academic success. But the "A" obviously can symbolize more. The student may feel pride and see in the "A" an image of his potentialities. His friends and fellow students may see still other meanings in the "A" and feel admiration or envy or scorn or a host of other possible sentiments.

The capacity to symbolize, to give meanings, cognitive and emotional, which we see in all of these illustrations, is a distinctively human capacity.

It was Cooley's significant insight that the sentiments that he saw as the core of human nature were not inherited. Rather, human nature develops in primary groups,

those simple face-to-face groups that are somewhat alike in all societies; groups of the family, the playground, and the neighborhood. In the essential similarity of these is to be found the basis, in experience, for similar ideas and sentiments in the human mind. In these, everywhere, human nature comes into existence. Man does not have it at birth; he cannot acquire it except through fellowship, and it decays in isolation.[2]

Although Cooley's insight (based in part on observation of his own children) perhaps outran the evidence then available to support it, several lines of more recent evidence tend to support and amplify his view. In various ways, they indicate that human nature is a product of involvement with other human beings.

Isolated Children

Numerous reports have been published of children reared in modern society but in relative isolation. The best-authenticated cases are those of Anna and Isabelle.[3] Anna was an illegitimate child, confined to one room from infancy. She had very little contact with other human beings. The mother brought her milk but otherwise paid little attention to her, not ordinarily taking the trouble to bathe, train, supervise, or cuddle her. When Anna was found, at the age of six, she showed few, if any, signs of human nature. She was described as completely apathetic; she lay on her back, immobile, expressionless, and indifferent. She was believed to be deaf and possibly blind. She lived for another five years, first in a country home and later in a foster home and school for retarded children, and in this period developed only to the level of the normal two-year-old. Whether the lack of development was due primarily to mental deficiency, to the deprivations of early life, or a combination of the two is not clear.

Isabelle's circumstances were relatively more fortunate. She, too, was an illegitimate child kept in seclusion. However, her deaf-mute mother was shut off with her, and the two were able to communicate by gestures. When Isabelle was found, also at the age of six, she, too, lacked a manifest human nature. She seemed utterly unaware of ordinary social relationships and reacted to strangers almost as an animal would, with fear and hostility. She made only a strange croaking sound, and in many respects her actions resembled those of deaf children. In contrast to Anna, Isabelle was given a systematic and skillful program of training and, after a very slow beginning, began to develop quite rapidly. By the time she was eight and a half years old, she had reached a normal educational level and was described as bright, cheerful, and energetic. Thus, with an appropriate environment she was able to develop into a girl with normal habits and feelings. That Isabelle attained this level of socialization indicates that she had an adequate intelligence potential, but only intensive and focused social interaction brought it to actuality. It is significant that Isabelle, in contrast to Anna, did have close, although limited, human contact when she was a baby.

Another case, reported from India, tells of a so-called feral child, a child who had been separated from society when still a baby and allegedly reared by wolves.[4] The child was about eight years old when, in 1921, she was discovered in a cave by a British missionary, and she lived for over eight years in the missionary school. When found, Kamala, as she was named, had few human characteristics. She wore no clothing, ate raw meat, lowered her mouth to her food, had impassive facial features, and showed only hostility to human beings. During her stay at the school Kamala never reached a normal level for her age, but she did make considerable progress, especially after she developed an emotional attachment to the missionary's wife. She learned to eat cooked food, to wear a dress, to understand simple language, to like other children, and to express various kinds of emotion. An analysis by Bruno Bettelheim strongly suggests that the wolf-rearing part of the story is a myth,[5] but without doubt Kamala had suffered extreme emotional isolation. To use Cooley's term, Kamala had no human nature when she was found; she developed it in the close personal contacts of the missionary school.

Deprivation in Social Relations

A second type of evidence comes from psychiatry. Many instances have been reported of children who, though not literally isolated from society, received as infants little attention and affection and did not establish any strong interpersonal ties or primary relationships with other human beings. In some cases they had a succession of ministering adults; in others they were in custodial institutions in which there were few adults to look after them. A growing body of evidence indicates that these children suffer from fundamental deprivation that prevents them from becoming adequately socialized.

Perhaps the best-known investigation of this problem is that of René Spitz, who reports on an institution in which there were ninety-one children, none older than three.[6] To take care of forty-five infants less than eighteen months old, there were only six nurses. For most of the day these infants lay on their backs in small cubicles, without human contact. Within the first year the average score of all the children on developmental tests fell from 124 to 72. Two years later a follow-up study found that over one-third of the ninety-one children had died, and the twenty-one who were still at the institution were extraordinarily retarded, even though the institution provided adequate nutrition and medical care. Despite the fact that conditions became much more favorable for children when they reached fifteen months, with more nurses and more opportunities for joint play activity, their heights and weights were below average, many could not walk or use a spoon, only one could dress himself, and only two had a vocabulary of more than five words. Spitz concludes that the conditions during the children's first year of life were so detrimental both physically and psychologically that the subsequent more favorable conditions could not counteract the damage.

These studies, as well as many others resulting in convergent findings, are instructive. They show that social isolation affects the biological process of maturation and even biological survival, as well as the socialization process. To grow into a human being—which is to say, to be capable of the sentiments that enable appropriate responsiveness to others—a baby must be treated like a human being; he must receive not just medically adequate physical care but "social care" as well.

The clinical investigations of psychiatrists on human children receive some support from two recent lines of research in related fields. One is Harry P. Harlow's study of rhesus monkeys. Now admittedly, it seems paradoxical to draw support for a view of human nature from observation of monkeys, but such evidence is relevant under certain conditions. If the observed behavior of monkeys has no parallel in human behavior, there is no justification for inferring from monkey behavior to that of humans. If, on the other hand, observations have been made on humans and conclusions drawn from them, then convergent findings on primates lower in the evolutionary scale tend to give support to those on humans. Such is the case with regard to the importance of social contact for development.

Harlow and his co-workers have carried out various experiments involving separation of newborn monkeys from their mothers, sometimes supplying "surrogate mothers." One type of surrogate mother is made simply of wire with a lactating nipple from which the monkey can feed; the other type is similar except that it is covered with cloth. Harlow finds that infants raised with a pair of artificial mothers, one wire and one cloth-covered, spend most of their time in contact with the cloth figure even if feeding from the wire one. When experimental monkeys become adult and mothers themselves, those reared only with a wire mother substitute tend to be either more aggressive or more indifferent toward their offspring than those raised with a cloth substitute. Such "mistreatment" of offspring—a "mistreatment" which may go so far as killing the babies—is also more likely among mothers reared without other monkeys in the same cage, as compared with mothers caged with peers during infancy. Various kinds of isolation make monkeys less "social" in their world. The development of an adequate "monkey nature" requires that the infant be reared in association with others of its species and that it have gratifying tactile experience.[7] This evidence converges with that concerning human infants.

The second recent line of research deals with "sensory deprivation" in human adults. Various experiments are being carried out to discover the effects of drastically reduced sensory stimulation. For example, one experimental arrangement involves having the person lie twenty-four hours a day on a comfortable bed in a lighted, semi-soundproof cubicle while wearing translucent goggles which admit diffuse light but prevent seeing patterns. Other arrangements may involve a darkened room or the wearing of heavy cotton gloves to reduce tactile stimulation. Although this line of investigation is still in its early stages, initial findings tend to converge with what we have already described. When people are subjected to such severe restriction of stimulation as described above, they suffer what psychologists describe as "deterioration of normal ego-functioning." Both emotional and symbolization capacities are impaired. One research group found that:

Subjects slip into a dream-like transitional state between
sleeping and waking which makes coherent thinking difficult;
thoughts cannot be anchored in reality and the free flow of
fantasy is promoted. . . . There is little motivation to speak
in the absence of a reply, and fantasy about the experimenters
is unchecked. It is therefore not surprising that paranoid fears
arise, but the extent of such fears *is* surprising, suggesting rapid
breakdown of the perception of social reality, that is, in terms
of the normal subject-experimenter relationship.[8]

Results such as these suggest that another of the conditions for the attainment and maintenance of human nature is an appropriate level and variety of stimulation. When stimulation is reduced to a bare minimum or is made uninterruptedly uniform for long periods—as occurs during certain types of "brainwashing"—the consequence may reasonably be described as a partial loss of human nature in those who experience it.

Finally, we may note one other relevant line of work. Psychiatric investigation suggests that lack of adequate early primary relations is responsible for many psychopathic personalities. The psychopath is someone who is almost completely self-centered. His relations with others are superficial; he is quite incapable of caring for others or of establishing emotional ties with them. He seems to have no internalized standards of right and wrong, no feelings of guilt, and often shows a general lack of concern in situations that ordinarily arouse some emotional response. When this type of person becomes delinquent, rehabilitation is extremely difficult. In Cooley's perspective such psychopaths have never developed a real human nature, because they have never experienced adequate primary-group relationships.

In summary, then, a third precondition for socialization is an inchoate human nature which develops into abilities to empathize and to symbolize. These abilities, in turn, make possible the development of the complex sentiments which uniquely characterize human nature.

In the ordinary course of events, the preconditions for socialization are taken for granted; only in exceptional circumstances do they come to our attention. Nevertheless, the process of socialization can be understood only as taking place in a context defined by an ongoing society, an adequate biological inheritance, and a characteristic human nature.

3 The Processes of Socialization

Although it is sometimes useful to speak of *the* process of socialization, just as we speak of the process of urbanization or industrialization or bureaucratization or modernization, the fact is that each of these terms is no more than a convenience for certain purposes. Each points in a general direction and identifies certain large-scale effects. When we study these phenomena, we quickly become aware that each of these terms encompasses diverse events. Socialization is not a unitary phenomenon, but rather a term for a variety of processes. The relationships among these specific processes are by no means fully worked out and understood; a unified and comprehensive theory of socialization has yet to be achieved. Nevertheless, we shall try, in this chapter, to identify and discuss the major processes. In so doing, we must approach our topic from several angles of vision, each of which illuminates the subject in a somewhat different way. Our goal here will be to present a general "model" of socialization that is broadly applicable and independent of specific cultures.

To begin, recall our definition of socialization: the process by which someone learns the ways of a given society or social group so that he can function within it. By unraveling this definition, we can fashion a framework that helps us locate component processes of socialization. Learning involves change; it sometimes occurs through teaching, which entails communication; learning, teaching, and communicating take place in a medium of emotionally significant relationships. Succinctly, then, we may say that socialization

(1) involves developmental change in the organism,
(2) through communication,
(3) in emotionally significant relationships,
(4) which are shaped by social groupings of varying scope.

It will be convenient to begin with the last point and move through the framework in reverse order.

Society and Socialization

Most commonly, socialization processes have been considered in face-to-face contexts such as the family, school, or peer group. Indeed, we shall focus on these contexts in Chapter 5. Yet it is clear that such groupings are agencies of the larger society. Parents do not raise their children to function only in the family but prepare them to leave the family and function in other settings. The school does the same. The values and techniques of peer-group relationships, although less obvious, likewise have their long-run applications. Furthermore, although families, schools, and other social groupings often direct divergent expectations toward those being socialized, they also often have convergent expectations. From this perspective, then, it is reasonable to say that *society specifies certain outcomes or ranges of outcomes of socialization*. For example, every society expends some of its resources to produce children who will become law-abiding adults. Children who do not become law-abiding are likely to be judged socialization failures. Another socialization outcome specified by the society is loyalty. The society seeks to engender loyalty to itself, and its various institutions and groups contribute to this outcome in various ways, Other types of outcomes and the concept of range of outcome will be discussed and illustrated shortly.

Families, schools, peer groups, and other agencies of socialization may vary in how attentive they are to socially desired outcomes, how they go about trying to bring about these outcomes, and how effective their chosen procedures are. Despite these variations, we can say that society—any society—endeavors to bring about certain desired and recognizable results in the socialization of its young. (Indeed, at various times society "gives recognition" when the desired results have been achieved—recognition in the form of titles, badges, diplomas, promotions, and so forth.)

The most basic result sought is a *motivated commitment to sustain responsive participation in society.* Another way to put this is to say that the child should become a person who recognizes and accepts legitimate claims made upon him by others. These claims are multiple and diverse, and they differ according to a person's location in the social structure. Some, however, are general. For example, the person should accept and function within the limits of communication and emotional expression that are defined as appropriate in different situations. Thus, he may scream at a football game, but not in a supermarket. He may laugh at home, at a movie, at a party, but not at a funeral. Another general type of claim may be expressed in this way: The person should accept the obligations of his roles. If he takes a job, he should do the work and meet its other legitimate requirements. If he enters into a friendship, he should be friendly according to the norms of that particular friendship, whatever they may be.

Even in those special cases where people are later trained for patterned withdrawal from general society—for example, nuns or monks who take vows of silence—the pattern of behavior is responsive to certain norms. It is not idiosyncratic withdrawal. Such an outcome falls within the range of socially acceptable results of socialization; although it represents a deviant role, it is not defined as a lack of motivated commitment to sustain responsive participation in society. In contrast, the role of "acid head"—the frequent taking of the drug LSD which induces hallucinations—is one type of "dropping out" of society. By definition, this behavior represents a failure of socialization from the perspective in which we are now viewing socialization.

The difference between the role of the monk who takes vows of silence and that of the acid head can be understood more fully by stating another socially specified outcome. As has been pointed out by sociologist Alex Inkeles[1] and social psychologist M. Brewster Smith,[2] society expects the development of some kind of *competence.* Different societies require different kinds of competence, and any one society requires different kinds of competence for its diverse social roles. Nevertheless, it seems possible to formulate certain general requirements that transcend this diversity. Inkeles does so in the following way:

Every individual must learn to be reasonably responsive to the pattern of social order and to the personal needs and requirements of the other individuals with whom he is in immediate contact. In other words, he must be basically socially conforming. He must have the ability to orient himself in space and time and have sufficient command of the rudimentary physical requirements of his setting so as not to destroy himself or be an undue burden on others. The requirements of society and of its specific statuses seem usually to involve certain motor and mental skills and techniques, and some kind of specialized knowledge and information; certain ways of thinking about the world, organized in a set of opinions and attitudes and constituting a distinctive idea system; a set of goals or values to guide action, and beliefs about the appropriate and acceptable paths to the goals; a conception of oneself which gives an identity and forms the basis for a system of social relations which include distinctive ways of relating to immediate authority, to intimates and peers, and to the larger community;

some pattern for the organization of psychic functioning which favors and facilitates certain distinctive modes of defense or moral functioning; and a particular cognitive, conative, and affective style.[3]

Applying this conception to our example, we may say that our society recognizes certain kinds of "religious competence" and allows the development of institutions in which that competence may be practiced, even when that practice takes the form of withdrawal from verbal communication in order to engage in meditation. In contrast, taking "trips" on "acid"— that is, engaging in drug-induced hallucinations—is defined by our society as willful destruction of a person's social competence and is therefore not generally accepted as a legitimate outcome of socialization in this society.

Now it is necessary here to introduce certain modifications of what has just been said. We have argued that many groups in a society have convergent expectations; that is, in any given society, family, school, church, and youth group, for example, press toward the same general outcomes. Because there is such convergence, we are justified in saying that society specifies certain outcomes. But two important modifications need to be stated: First, the fact that various institutions in a society tend to be mutually supportive in what they expect does not mean that they are entirely so. There is conflict between institutions as well as support. Parents often do not approve of what the school does, and vice versa. Accordingly, socialization is not a smooth process. The child is subjected to conflicting expectations as well as mutually supportive ones.

Second, in arguing that society seeks to generate a motivated commitment to sustain social participation and certain general forms of competence, we ignored certain phenomena that also are among the processes of socialization. Earlier we spoke of "dropping out" as a failure of socialization. What needs to be added here is that whereas some socialization failures may be attributable to particular socializing agents, other failures may be due to society's own organization. Thus, society may expect all children to learn certain things but may order its institutions in such a way that some are prevented from learning what they are expected to learn. In the United States, for example, one of the goals of the elementary school is to teach children how to get along with others. But many institutional arrangements have resulted in segregating whites from blacks in their schooling, so that there is a systematically fostered limiting of competence. To take another example: As this book is being written, there has been a "rediscovery" of hunger and malnutrition in various sections of the United States. Political and economic institutions do not deliver food to all who need it, and many suffer from malnutrition. These nutritional deficiencies very likely impair mental ability and thus prevent children from learning things they are expected to learn.[4] This again is an example of how the pattern of institutions can generate failures in socialization. More generally, although every society expects various types of minimal competence and seeks to foster more than minimal competence in those activities it most values, no society succeeds in eliciting even minimal levels among all its children, in part because the institutional pattern interferes.

These, then, are the two general goals of socialization: a motivated *commitment* to sustain responsive participation in society and forms of *competence* that the society accepts as appropriate. These goals are generic; they are universally applicable. Of course, when we become more specific, we find that the same kinds of commitment and competence are not expected of all members of society. The artist and the career soldier differ not only in their kinds of competence but also in the kinds of commitment to social participation expected of them. The soldier will participate in a set of relationships governed by rigid rules of obedience to command. The artist will participate in a set of relationships governed by efforts to attract an audience that will appreciate the uniqueness of his vision and his skill. It is beyond the scope of this book to attempt to explain how the socialization process makes career soldiers of some and artists of others. What can be said here from this example, however, is that society expects the socialization process to enable every new member eventually to find *some* appropriate adult status(es) within some legitimate set(s) of relationships. As we noted in Chapter 2, each status entails a role. On the basis of our present discussion we can add that a role (such as the occupational role of soldier or artist) involves a particular type of commitment to social participation and a particular type of competence.

Of course, while socialization is expected to result in the fulfilling of various specialized roles, it must also, as Inkeles points out, make it possible for the person to participate in a variety of ways with others whose statuses and roles are quite different from his own. Robert Hutchins, former president of the University of Chicago, used to deride a certain engineering school that maintained a Department of Engineering English because, as he put it, "nobody else talks engineering English." Whatever the merit of his derisiveness, the point he was making was that socialization can sometimes result in such an intense commitment to a particular form of social participation as to hamper social participation across role boundaries. A similar point had been made earlier by social critic and economist Thorstein Veblen, who spoke of a "trained incapacity."

Any society provides a variety of statuses and roles. Usually it also has more or less explicit rules governing access to at least certain statuses and roles. The social class into which a child is born may decisively determine the statuses and roles open to him in later life. As early as 1944, W. Lloyd Warner and his colleagues showed that the type of education young American children receive is determined to a large extent by their social class.[5] Their conclusions have been borne out by much subsequent investigation. Ethnic group membership and religion are often decisive determinants of the kinds of social participation that will be allowed and the kinds of competence that children will be able to acquire. Thus, for example, blacks in the United States, French Canadians in Canada, Slovaks in Czechoslovakia, Indians in Latin American countries, Catholics in Northern Ireland and, until recent times, Jews in many countries have been restricted in certain kinds of social participation and often prevented from gaining the kinds of competence the societies value most highly. These groups have, in their respective societies, been depreciated by more dominant groups who have effective control of many institutions including, importantly, the schools, which affect socialization outcomes. With more or less stringency, the children of these depreciated groups have been socialized toward the less valued statuses and roles, often toward those that sociologist Everett Hughes has characterized as the "dirty work" of the society. Conversely, children born into more favored segments of society are socialized toward more favored statuses and roles. Generally, then, we may say that society has criteria for distinguishing among children and procedures for directing different groups of children into different sequences of experiences which eventuate in different socialization outcomes. These criteria are often based upon status attributes of the family into which the child is born.

Thus we see that society organizes itself in such a way as to develop in its children both a general commitment to participate in society and a general competence for doing so, and also a variety of commitments and competences that are considered relevant to particular statuses and roles. Our examples of the last point have been drawn from the realm of occupations, but we must now consider an aspect of commitment and competence that is more general than the occupational. One criterion by which every society differentiates socialization outcomes is sex. There is no society that does not expect differences in social participation and competence from males and females, differences that are summed up in the sociological term *sex role.*

Although sex-role expectations are, of course, *based on* anatomy, physiology, and such other biological differences as physical strength and endurance, they are not fully *determined by* these biological factors. Sigmund Freud, the originator of psychoanalysis, once wrote that "anatomy is destiny"; this is true, but not entirely in the way Freud meant it. For, while he saw sexual biology as determinative of the person's psychological outlook and life course, contemporary knowledge gained by anthropology and sociology reveals that society shapes sex roles more than Freud recognized. True, there are at least a few biologically determined universals; no society attempts to socialize males to become mothers. However, contemporary psychoanalyst Bruno Bettelheim argues that this is not because males don't want to be mothers. On the contrary, he argues that males are often envious of women's capacity to bear children and that the rites of puberty for males found in many preliterate societies are in fact not merely socialization into a male role but socialization away from a female role. Such rites often involve inflicting scars, and Bettelheim interprets these as symbolic equivalents of the pains of childbearing.[6] Far-fetched as this interpretation may seem, it affords a curious and subtle support for the sociological interpretation of sex roles. For, along with its insistence on the basic fatefulness of sexual anatomy, psychoanalysis also holds that humans are basically bisexual in their impulses and that socialization must and does lead to suppression of impulses that are inappropriate to the person's anatomical sex.

Bettelheim's analysis, which may or may not be correct, is not widely accepted, but it is of interest here in suggesting how significant and far-reaching the socialization process is. Society defines the biological distinction between maleness and femaleness as fundamental and builds an elaborate array of expectations upon it, expectations that go far beyond and have no connection with the different biological functions in procreation. Most societies, for example, prescribe different kinds of work as suitable for males and females. Although these work distinctions are sometimes related to differences in strength and endurance, often they are not. In the United States, for example, most dentists and doctors are men; in the Soviet Union, most are women.[7] This is the result of differences in social expectation and has no connection with innate biological capacities.

Societal expectations influence not only formal statuses and roles but expressive behavior, interests, and popular images as well. Men walk, talk, light matches, and cross their legs differently from women. Men are concerned with sports and politics, women with fashions and beauty products. Men are (or have been) expected and allowed to speak "more coarsely" than women, who are allowed and expected to be more sentimental and disposed to cry.

Aside from the influence of hereditary dispositions—and there is as yet no consensus on their relative significance—boys and girls come to learn their sex identities and expectations of behavior through differential observations, treatment, and emotional attachments. The girl is (or, at least, was until recently) given pink, the boy blue; the girl a doll carriage, and the boy a baseball glove. The boy is told to be brave, is complimented for throwing a ball well, may be locked out of the room when his mother is dressing, and is teased when his behavior seems too emotional. The girl is told to keep her dress down, is laughed at—or commended—for flirting, is admired for her curls, and is teased for acting like a tomboy. The child, in innumerable instances of everyday life has his behavior defined in sex-status terms and, in some way or another, is rewarded for appropriate behavior and ignored or punished for inappropriate behavior.

In recent years, considerable discussion has concerned the changing patterns of sex roles. Charles Winick, for example, has assembled a considerable array of evidence that suggests a blurring of sex-role identification in the United States, especially since World War II.[8] Urbanization, technical specialization, changing birth rates, the extension of education, the growth of the mass media, and a generally rising standard of living have all affected the behavior of men and women and the patterns of socialization. Sometimes sex-role expectations change in fairly direct response to changes in social institutions. Thus, as the industrial order requires increasingly higher levels of technical competence, the resultant strain on "manpower" available to fill such occupations results in greater acceptance of women. The woman engineer, chemist, or physicist is increasingly acceptable. On the other hand, sex-role changes also come about through opposition to the established institutional order. Thus, increasing bureaucratization has given rise to efforts to alter sex-role expectations that are congruent with a more highly organized society. Males now increasingly resist "the gray-flannel mentality" by asserting new norms of flamboyant dress and idiosyncratic hair styles. The analysis of these changes would take more space than is available here.

At this point, we must return to our general account and ask: How does society attempt to realize the outcomes it expects of socialization? To answer this question, we must now adopt some other angles of vision.

Emotionally Significant Relationships

Where does socialization begin? We have given one answer to this question by saying that society specifies desired outcomes that are to be brought about by its agencies—its families, schools, churches, youth groups, mass media, and other accepted institutions. From this perspective, socialization begins with the specification of outcomes toward which all newborns will be directed.

But the newborn, of course, knows nothing of this. If we look at the question from this perspective, it receives a different answer: Socialization begins with *personal attachment*. Born helpless, vocal but without speech, with only the potentiality to become human, needing care, the infant begins to be socialized by being cared for by one or more persons who are committed to caring for him. At birth, the child evokes sentiments of pride, love, tenderness, responsibility, hope, and so forth, in those who receive him as a new member of the group. Most important among them usually is the mother. She responds to him on the basis of the sentiments he evokes in her.[9] Her response has many aspects. She touches and holds the child in a certain way, perhaps self-confidently, perhaps apprehensively. She may be diligent or dilatory in responding to his cries. She may breast-feed and sing to him, or she may routinely give him a bottle and let him feed in solitude.

From the perspective of the individual child starting out in life, the mother-child relationship is where socialization begins. What happens in this relationship that initiates socialization? Many different things.

This is the infant's first relationship with another person. It is therefore his first significant encounter with what it means to be human. Being cared for is his first experience of social life. As such, and coming before he can evaluate it, the relationship with his mother is virtually all the social life he has and therefore presents him with his first expectation of the social world. The infant whose mother spends much time with him, singing, playing, feeding, will have a different expectation of social life than the infant whose mother gives only minimal care.

Not less important, in this first attachment the child has the beginnings of his sense of himself. One fundamental fact of the mother-child relationship is that the adult has far more power than the infant. But this is not to say that the infant is necessarily powerless, as is sometimes incorrectly stated. For in this situation the infant has the possibility of gaining some power. If his cries of discomfort succeed with some consistency in evoking parental response that allays the discomfort, then, we have reason to believe, he is launched on a path of experiencing himself as effective. On the other hand, when his cries do not bring response, or do so only inconsistently, his sense of powerlessness is intensified.

That the mother-child relationship is important for socialization has long been believed, but efforts to identify the crucial aspects of this relationship have met with uneven success. Psychoanalysis, a bold theory formulated on the basis of closely attentive observation of adults being treated for emotional disturbances, had argued that the child's earliest feelings about feeding and excreting were influential—often decisive—in shaping the child's later development. Academic research workers were challenged by this theory presented by nonacademic clinicians and sought to test these ideas in a way that would justify accepting or rejecting them. What was important about feeding? Was it the difference between breast-feeding and bottle-feeding? Was it the suddenness or gradualness of weaning? Since toilet training seemed to be the first clear imposition of society's demands upon the unsocialized infant, did the age at which such training was begun make a difference? And was it better to start early or late? Should the mother be gentle or stern in the way she went about it?

These and numerous related questions prompted a voluminous quantity of research. In a meticulous review of this research—a review which itself fills nearly eighty pages—Bettye M. Caldwell concludes that the results remain inconclusive.[10] The research does not justify the conclusion that feeding and toilet-training practices have no effect, but neither is it clear that the practices as such have definite effects.

A different kind of study, by Lois Murphy, suggests that whether or not the infant was orally *gratified* during the first six months of life is the more important issue.[11] According to her study, children who received much oral gratification during the first six months of life showed greater ability to cope with difficulties and frustrations at later preschool ages. The general explanation is that such gratification minimizes tension in the infant and thereby leaves him free to acquire a firmer sense of himself and of his environment. We shall return to these questions later. For present purposes it is sufficient to note that although the difference between breast-feeding and bottle-feeding appeared to make no difference to the infant's gratification, whether or not the mother allowed him to reject unwanted foods did make a difference in his later effectiveness. Since "allowing" is one way of establishing expectations in a relationship, Murphy's study provides some evidence that early experiences in the mother-child relationship give rise to expectations that influence later socialization.

That children form attachments even as early as three or four months is indicated in a study by Leon J. Yarrow. Infants of this age who were moved from foster homes to adoptive homes showed disturbances such as withdrawn behavior, increased apathy, and disturbances of sleep and feeding. "More overt social disturbances—excessive clinging or definite rejection of the new mother—occurred with increasing frequency after six months."[12]

In sum, by being cared for, by evoking response and being responded to, the infant obtains his first sense of himself, his first sense of another person, his first experience of a social relationship. In this relationship he develops his first expectations and thus his first sense of social order. A rudimentary temporal order emerges from such experiences as the interval between crying and being responded to; the interval between feedings; the alternation of sleeping and wakefulness. In being cared for, the infant has his first experiences of those sentiments which Cooley identified decades ago as the hallmark of human nature.

The child's attachment to the mother is the first of many emotionally significant relationships that he will form in the course of his life. (We have been assuming that the primary infant-care functions are largely carried out by a single person, the mother, which is the most usual situation. Some cultures, however, provide that such care is apportioned among several people. But even when this is the case, there is some evidence that the infant forms a closer attachment to one among the multiple mother figures.[13]) His socialization will be shaped by diverse attachments to a diversity of people, who will be for him his *significant others*: father, siblings, age-mates and older children in neighborhood and school, relatives, teachers, friends, and "enemies." He will form a somewhat different kind of relationship with each of these people; because of this, and because they each have a different status in society and a different role in relation to him, each will make a different kind of contribution to his socialization. These differences will give rise to problems for the child from an early age, with the conflict between parents and age-mates typically being a focus of stress. The four-year-old encouraged by his playmate to cross the street in pursuit of adventure may experience distress before he follows the suggestion or only after his parent has discovered that he has done so. In either case, he is experiencing an early form of the conflict of norms and expectations that impinge on him from socializing agents who occupy different statuses.

Communication

Now we face a paradox. Society presses toward certain outcomes, yet socialization begins in a two-person relationship of mother giving care to an infant who cannot speak or think or even understand instruction. How can an infant traverse the path from this beginning to that of a participating member of society? How can he be set upon this path?

The relevant facts here are that the speechless newborn can feel and he can communicate, and these resources can get him started. At the outset the infant can feel discomfort and comfort. When he feels discomfort, he cries. His mother hears the cry, *interprets* it as a sign of discomfort, and *responds* with activities that she hopes will restore the infant to comfort or at least keep him quiet. She will evaluate, or interpret, her own effort as successful when the child ceases to cry. Her initial efforts may not be "on target" because she may incorrectly interpret the source of the discomfort and the actions that will be effective in assuaging it. She may assume the child is hungry, only to find that he does not nurse. Further trial and error will lead to a "correct interpretation" —that is, one that leads the child to stop crying and leads the mother to judge that she has responded appropriately.

Symbols, Language, and Interaction

The situation we have just described is the prototype of social interaction from which more complex forms evolve and through which the infant will develop into a person who can function in society. In this rudimentary interaction, the child makes a sound that is not simply a noise to his mother. The noise is significant to her—on two bases. First, she accepts the noise as having a legitimate claim upon her attention, because of her relationship to the child. His cry will not go unnoticed as might the noise of an airplane passing overhead, because *for her* it signifies or *symbolizes her* attachment to him. It does so independently of how she chooses to respond to the cry. But the second meaning of the cry is a responsive or *interactive* meaning. She may decide that the cry should be interpreted as meaning she should attend to the infant right away. Alternatively, she may decide to interpret it as one that allows her to wait until a more convenient moment to respond. Or she may decide not to respond immediately, with the express goal of teaching the child to tolerate more discomfort. Whatever her particular response, she engages in an imaginative process—which may take no more than an instant—in which she represents to herself what the child is probably feeling and what should be done about it. Her overt response to the child's cry occurs only after the process of inner representation.

The capacity to interpret communications from others and to represent to oneself what others may think, feel, and do is fundamental to all of social life. The newborn does not have this capacity, and this is what he must develop. At the outset he experiences discomfort but does not know how it can be assuaged. His cry is involuntary; it is not a communication *to him.* But in time, as his cries succeed in bringing his mother and comfort, they begin to be more under his voluntary control. Whether he develops, in this pre-verbal period, the capacity to form mental representations of her is a moot question. Some psychoanalytic writers postulate that the pre-verbal infant does have the capacity to imagine his mother coming to him. Most scholars, including most psychoanalytic writers, remain skeptical because there is no reasonable way at this time to ascertain whether a pre-verbal infant does or does not imagine anything. Nevertheless, the child becomes increasingly able to anticipate his mother's appearance. By the time he becomes able to stand in his crib, he is also able to look toward the door through which his mother will enter and to greet her entry by rocking on his feet, reaching out, and changing his vocalization—before she ministers to him. He has developed some expectations that are responsive to the expectations his mother has as she comes to tend to him. He is on his way to becoming socialized. He begins to learn how to function in society by learning how to function in the relationship with his mother.

With the gradual acquisition of language, socialization accelerates and becomes qualitatively transformed from its pre-verbal beginnings. Language is, of course, part of the heritage of a society, and facility in the use of its language is one of the kinds of competence toward which society directs its newborns. But while *language facility* is one of the expected outcomes of socialization, *language acquisition* is of enormous importance as one of the component processes of socialization long before full facility is achieved.

Recall our account of mother-infant interaction. When the infant cries, his mother interprets it as a sign of need. But she must discover for herself whether he is hungry, wet, cold, has caught his foot in the slats of the crib or is in some other state of discomfort. His cry is an interpretable symbol to his mother but only imperfectly so; and it is not at all a symbol to the infant.[14] As he acquires the ability to use common gestures and language, he is acquiring the ability to symbolize—the ability to identify and name things, people, and feelings. In place of a nonspecific cry, he is able to point or tug or name his wish to another. But in order to be able to do this, he has to be able to identify it to himself. When the child is able to present to himself the same symbol for an object that he presents to others, he has taken a large step toward regulating his own behavior and simultaneously a large step toward participating responsively with others. A qualitative change of great importance has thus taken place when, instead of a nonspecific cry, the child can designate his wishes with words that communicate specifically: "bottle," "wet," "pick me up," and so on. He now has at his disposal specific symbols whose meaning *he knows* and which he knows his mother knows. He is entering into a social world of shared symbols. His capacity for social interaction is thus expanding enormously as he masters an expanding array of shared symbols. In this process he is gaining the capacity to move beyond the circumscribed world of the mother-child relationship into a larger social world of widely shared symbols.

Recent research on the acquisition of language indicates that it is a far more complicated process than had previously been supposed.[15] Indeed, like socialization generally, it involves many component processes. Two deserve brief mention here. From one point of view, language consists of words, and learning language involves learning words. An infant begins to speak by making random sounds. When he makes a sound that approximates a word in his "native language," his parents and others encourage him by repeating the sound as the "correct word" which they almost hear. By responding in an interested and pleasurable way and by providing the child with "correct pronunciations" of words they imagine he is struggling to say, the child's significant others reward and encourage his further efforts. Since much of this activity goes on in relation to specific objects and experiences in the child's world, the random sounds develop into both "real words" and into symbols for objects and experiences. Sound and meaning come to be associated.

This view of language learning has been held for some time. It seems satisfactory as far as it goes, but it doesn't go far enough. A number of linguistic scholars, most prominently Noam Chomsky, have pointed out that language consists not simply of words but of sentences.[16] Further, there is no limit to the number of sentences that can be formed. Even a child will, at some point, begin to speak sentences he has never heard before and which therefore cannot be explained simply as the result of his being directly taught in the fashion described in the preceding paragraph. Accordingly, these scholars argue, in some fashion the child learns *"productive rules* that enable the speaker to produce the infinite variety of sentences that he produces and to understand the infinite variety of sentences that he hears."[17] How the child learns these rules is not yet understood, but more is involved than learning textbook grammar. The available evidence does indicate, according to James J. Jenkins, that

the child is very systematic in his approach to language. It may be that he moves from one system to another, testing, changing, testing, trying again, or it may be that he chooses one system and progressively differentiates it into finer and finer portions; but the evidence that he is doing *something* systematic is overwhelming. . . . there is evidence that the child is struggling with a system for generating language at every stage and in very complex ways.[18]

These insights into the child's learning of language emphasize that in the course of socialization he is engaged in an effort to develop an inner regulation of his behavior, an internal order that in some adequate way corresponds to an external social order.

Language is, then, an example of social order, just as the arrangement of houses on streets or the exchange of money for goods and services are examples of social order. All three regulate the relationships among people in accordance with rules, and the child will have to learn the relevant rules for these and many other aspects of social order.

But language plays a particularly significant part in organizing a social order and in the child's socialization into that order. Language is, among its other functions, a system for classifying objects and events in ways that are socially significant. Thus, if a child sits on a table, he may be told "that's not a chair." The table surface lends itself to sitting just as does the seat of a chair; but despite their physical similarity in this respect they are socially defined as totally different objects, and this difference is embodied in a verbal classification that organizes behavior in relation to the objects. The way in which things and events are verbally classified defines their social nature, and these classifications become a fundamental part of our way of thinking and acting. Our very perception is shaped by our language categories. In time the child will not even see the table as offering the possibility for sitting, because his knowledge of it as being within the category "table" will preclude the possibility.

Categorization of social reality takes more complex forms. A common example in our society is the disposition to see many situations in "either-or" terms. The child may encounter this at the dinner table in the form of "Either eat your vegetables or go without dessert." Another situation of similar form is "Practice the piano (do your homework, clean up your room) or you can't go out to play." Desired activities are thus often incorporated in an "either-or" way of thinking that makes them contingent on the performance of some undesired activity—"or else."

Finally, one further indication of the way in which language shapes experience is of particular interest. Freud called attention to "the peculiar amnesia which veils from most people (not from all) the first years of their childhood, usually the first six or eight years."[19] He was impressed with the fact that childhood experiences are often vivid and that they include love, jealousy, and other passions. Yet despite the intensity, memories of these experiences in later years are fragmentary at best. Following up Freud's observations, but dissatisfied with his explanation of this massive failure of memory, Ernest G. Schachtel proposed the following explanation: Memory organizes past experiences in the service of present needs, fears, and interests. Adult memory is organized into categories that are shaped by society. These categories, he argues, "are not suitable vehicles to receive and reproduce experiences of the quality and intensity typical of early childhood," because they are shaped by the biases, emphases, and taboos of adult culture. Adult memory is essentially conventionalized, and therefore early childhood experience—in which everything seems new, fresh, and exciting—is incompatible, hence forgotten. The conventionalization of memory proceeds so far that, as Schachtel puts it:

... the memories of the majority of people come to resemble increasingly the stereotyped answers to a questionnaire, in which life consists of time and place of birth, religious denomination, residence, educational degrees, job, marriage, number and birthdates of children, income, sickness and death. ... the average traveler through life remembers chiefly ... what he is supposed to remember because it is exactly what everybody else remembers too. ... Experience increasingly assumes the form of the cliché under which it will be recalled. ... This is not the remembered situation itself but the words which are customarily used to indicate this situation and the reactions which it is supposed to evoke. ... There are people who experience a party, a visit to the movies, a play, a concert, a trip in the very words in which they are going to tell their friends about it; in fact, quite often they anticipate such experience in these words. The experience is predigested, as it were, even before they have tasted of it. Like the unfortunate Midas, whose touch turned everything into gold so that he could not eat or drink, these people turn the potential nourishment of the anticipated experience into the sterile currency of the conventional phrase which exhausts their experience because they have seen, heard, felt nothing but this phrase with which later they will report to their friends the "exciting time" they have had.[20]

Thus, Schachtel maintains, language not only shapes memory into conventionalized categories; in extreme cases it even conventionalizes the experience before it passes into memory. But even in ordinary cases, conventionalization is so powerful that most early childhood experience is not accessible to memory.

The Significance of Significant Others

With our discussion of emotional attachments and of communication as background, we are now in a position to identify some additional processes that make significant others significant to the child and that help him develop from the primarily biological organism he is at birth into a person as well.

When we say that the task of socialization is to enable the child to learn to function in society, we refer to a complex type of adaptation that cannot be understood as a kind of mechanical conformity. As our brief sketch of man's biological nature in Chapter 2 makes clear, human socialized behavior is not analogous to the behavior of the trained rat running a maze and receiving rewards for making correct turns in correct sequence. (The fundamental dissimilarity is conveyed by the expression "rat race," referring to a pattern of life that is too dominated by pursuit of externally set goals in conformity with rigidly specified rules. To call this life pattern a rat race is to criticize it as departing too far from human nature.)

Socialization is, then, not simply a process of making correct motions prescribed by trainers. Running in a rat race or jumping through a hoop are, when applied to humans, terms for caricaturing certain distortions of socialization.

As suggested by our discussion of learning language rules, the essence of socialization is the person's *internal regulation* of his own behavior in ways that are adequate to the interpersonal situations and to the larger social order in which he participates. The capability for internal regulation develops as a result of interaction with significant others.

Significant others present themselves to the child in two essential ways:

1. By what they do
2. By what they say (and how they say it)

Doing and saying are, of course, organized in terms of roles. Thus, a mother presents herself to her child by feeding, changing his diaper, offering him toys, addressing him with words of endearment. His older brother throws a ball, climbs trees, and uses a different vocabulary. His father carries a toolbox or a briefcase, watches football games, and uses yet another vocabulary.

As the infant becomes aware of the activities going on around him, he becomes interested in them; and because they are the activities of people to whom he is emotionally attached, he wants to do what they do and, indeed, to be as they are. For example, not long after a mother begins giving her child nonliquid food, the child wishes to feed her as he is being fed. He tries to take the spoon from her and feed her. As the range of his observation expands, he tries other activities which seem interesting: turning light switches on and off, opening the refrigerator, and the like. And while his significant others are engaged in such activities, they are also engaged in saying things—naming the objects they handle, describing what they are doing ("Here's your doll."), playing word games ("Where's your nose? Show me your nose.").

The child begins to repeat the words he hears and to carry out the actions he sees others carry out. In short, he perceives his significant others as *role models*. They provide the patterns of behavior and conduct on which he patterns himself. It is through interaction with these role models that the child develops the ability to regulate his own behavior.

The basic fact that the child's regulation of his own behavior develops from interaction with role models has been noted by numerous interpreters but explained variously by them. No single account of this process and its consequences is fully satisfactory, nor has anyone yet developed a satisfactory composite interpretation. We shall therefore draw upon several sources that seem necessary for an adequate understanding of this process but which do not yet fit well together.

For George Herbert Mead, an influential figure in American sociology though not himself a sociologist, the principal outcome of socialization that makes self-regulation possible is the development of the *self*. The self, in his view, is the capacity to represent to oneself what one wishes to communicate to others. Language plays a crucial part in development of the self. This is why, from Mead's point of view, the child's change from simply crying to being able to use socially shared symbols such as "I want bottle," "Go outside" (for "I want to go outside") is such a significant transformation.[21] Only humans can self-consciously and purposively represent to themselves that which they wish to represent to others; this, for Mead, is what it means to have a self and what it means to be human. The child who can do this is on his way to becoming human, that is, to being simultaneously self-regulating and socially responsive.

In addition to language, which he considers paramount, Mead also recognizes the importance of the child's observations of others' activities. He postulated that the child goes through two stages of observation toward the development of his self. In the first, or *play stage*, the child takes the roles of others: He plays at being the others who are significant to him. He wants to push the broom, carry the umbrella, put on the hat, and do all the other things he sees his parents do, including saying what they say. The story is told of the four-year-old playing "Daddy" who put on his hat and coat, said "Good-bye," and walked out the front door, only to return a few minutes later because he didn't know what to do next. He had taken as much of his father's work role as he could see and hear—the ritualized morning departure. What is noteworthy in this illustration (as in all play) is that the child is now able to govern his own behavior to a certain extent. When he first heard adults say "bye-bye" to him, he did nothing because the sound had no meaning to him. Nor did it mean anything when he first learned to repeat the sound. Now when he says "Good-bye," he directs himself to walk out the door.

In the play stage the child plays at many roles that offer interesting models to him, not only imitating his parents and other children but also playing "cops and robbers," postman, space pilot, and so on, ad infinitum. During this stage he progresses to taking two complementary roles at a time. Thus, he may say things to himself that his mother has said to him, then reply in his own role of child. If no playmates are around, he may enact the roles of both cop and robber in alternation.

With further development the child enters the *game stage*. The importance of this lies in the fact that games involve an organization of roles, and the child participating has to take the role of everyone else. In Mead's famous example of the baseball game, the child

must have the responses of each position involved in his own position. He must know what everyone else is going to do in order to carry out his own play. He has to take all of these roles. They do not all have to be present in consciousness at the same time, but at some moments he has to have three or four individuals present in his own attitude, such as the one who is going to throw the ball, the one who is going to catch it, and so on. These responses must be, in some degree, present in his own make-up. In the game, then, there is a set of responses of such others so organized that the attitude of one calls out the appropriate attitudes of the other.[22]

Then, as Mead puts it:

This getting of the broad activities of any given social whole or organized society as such within the experiential field of any one of the individuals involved . . . is . . . the essential basis and prerequisite of the fullest development of that individual's self: only in so far as he takes the attitudes of the organized social group to which he belongs toward the organized, co-operative social activity or set of such activities in which that group . . . is engaged, does he develop a complete self. . . . And on the other hand, the complex co-operative processes and activities and institutional functionings of organized human society are also possible only in so far as every individual involved in them . . . can take the general attitudes of all other such individuals with reference to these processes and activities and institutional functionings, and to the organized social whole of experiential relations and interactions thereby constituted —and can direct his own behavior accordingly.[23]

Mead's explanation of the development of the self, shaped by language and role taking, remains one of the basic building blocks in our understanding of how man functions in society. In certain respects it is unexcelled to this day, more than forty years after his death. But it contains some important omissions. For example, Mead does not distinguish among different kinds of utterance. His approach finds no significance in the difference between a parent's saying "Here's your ball" and "Don't do that!" The latter expression is important in ways that the former is not, even though both are statements made by the same role model and both help the child to categorize the world in linguistic terms. But the latter statement is made *authoritatively*. It is more than a simple categorization. It is a statement of a *rule*, and it carries with it the suggestion of a *sanction*.

Role models who can present themselves to the child with authority to state rules and to enforce them with positive and negative sanctions play a particularly decisive part in the development of the child's self. An admired uncle who pilots a plane may catch the child's imagination more than his own father who works at a nine-to-five desk job. But the father, as the model who wields the more effective authority over the child's life, is likely to have greater influence in shaping the child's social participation. He, along with the mother, makes the child aware of limits to acceptable behavior. In short, the child has impulses and attempts actions that are unacceptable to those who have effective authority to interpret his behavior in the light of norms and values and to offer rewards and impose penalties to encourage appropriate conduct. (Effective authority does not rest only with adults. When the child plays with his peers, he comes under a system of norms and sanctions that define "playing fair" and "cheating.") The self is established, then, not only on the basis of taking the role of the other but also through the process of *internalizing the values and norms* that are effectively presented by authoritative role models. In one sense socialization can be summed up by saying that what was once outside the individual comes to be inside him. Society comes to exist within the individual as well as outside of him. This is the developmental change that makes all the difference.

But we must consider developmental change from another angle of vision as well.

Socialization and Time

Socialization is an extended process. It takes time, obviously. Less obviously, it takes different kinds of time. To begin, let us make a basic distinction between *life-cycle time* and *social time*, after which we shall note some of their complexities.

By life-cycle time we mean a sequence of biological stages determined by maturation. Everywhere humans are born small and helpless. They then pass through a decade and a half or so of increasing strength. Sometime during the second decade puberty is reached and sexual maturity attained. For several decades thereafter, adult levels of energy are sustained, followed by a period of more or less precipitous decline. This sequence of stages is universal. The age at which changes occur varies according to many influences, but the sequence itself is not alterable.

Social time may be generally defined as the organization of events into socially meaningful units. As society changes, the organization of time is likely to change. For example, when people worked a six-day week, they had one day of rest called the Sabbath. With a five-day work week now standard, the nonwork unit is of two days' duration and is called the weekend, although it could conceivably have been called "double Sabbath." The weekend is not simply twice as long as the Sabbath but is very different in social meaning as well.

Every society, in organizing its social life, takes note of the biological stages, a phenomenon known as *age grading*. Age grading is thus one type of social time. But every society does not make the same age distinctions, nor does every society consider them of equal importance. Furthermore, as a society changes, its age grading is also likely to change. Thus it may be said that the biological life cycle constitutes a substratum upon which society imposes its own distinctions as an overlay.

Social change is relevant to socialization. We discover from the work of Philippe Ariès, a sociologically minded historian, that the very notion of a distinctive period of life conceived of as childhood is of fairly recent origin. The many facts of childhood that seem so compellingly distinctive to us and lead us to differentiate the early years from those that follow did not have this impact in Western countries before about the sixteenth century. This was shown in many ways in earlier times. For example, once the infant was out of swaddling clothes, he was dressed just like "the other men and women" of his social class; there was no distinctive dress for children in medieval society. After the age of three or four, children played the same games as adults, including card games and games of chance for money. Documents from the early seventeenth century reveal that adults did not refrain from gestures and jokes with children that would today be regarded as immoral or perverted. Ariès notes:

> In medieval society, the idea of childhood did not exist; this is not to suggest that children were neglected, forsaken or despised. The idea of childhood is not to be confused with affection for children; it corresponds to an awareness of the particular nature of childhood . . . which distinguishes the child from the adult, even the young adult. In medieval society, this awareness was lacking. . . .
>   In the Middle Ages, at the beginning of modern times, and for a long time after that in the lower classes, children were mixed with adults as soon as they were considered capable of doing without their mothers or nannies, not long after a tardy weaning (in other words about the age of seven). They immediately went straight into the great community of men, sharing in the work and play of their companions, old and young alike. The movement of collective life carried in a single torrent all ages and classes.[24]

The awareness of childhood as a distinct period of life is, then, a historical creation. Once this awareness developed, the nature of childhood and what should be done about it became a matter of ideological controversy, and it has remained so down to our time. At some periods and among some groups, the child has been regarded as basically tender and innocent. In opposition to this has been the notion that he is wild and needs to be tamed. These two images continue to have their respective adherents.

Within any given society in a given historical period, the child passes through various kinds of sequences. Ariès describes how the school year has become a time unit for socialization:

> Today the class, the constituent cell of the school structure, presents certain precise characteristics which are entirely

familiar: it corresponds to a stage in the progressive acquisition of knowledge (to a curriculum), to an average age from which every attempt is made not to depart, to a physical spatial unit, for each age group and subject group has its special premises . . . and to a period of time, an annual period at the end of which the class's complement changes.

The extremely close connection between the age of the pupils and the organic structure which gathers them together gives each year a personality of its own: the child has the same age as his class, and each class acquires from its curriculum, its classroom and its master a distinctive complexion. The result is a striking differentiation between age groups which are really quite close together. The child changes his age every year at the same time as he changes his class. In the past, the span of life and childhood was not cut up into such thin slices. The school class has thus become a determining factor in the process of differentiating the ages of childhood and early adolescence.[25]

Of course, while the child is passing through these school-determined age statuses, each with its own contribution to socialization, he is also passing through other gradations that are not institutionally determined or precisely delineated but which nevertheless mark significant steps. Such distinctions are numerous: for example, the progression from the play to the game stage in Mead's analysis. Or consider the progression from being a child who must come in when it gets dark to one who is allowed to stay out after dark with peers; or the farm child old enough for his own pony, the city child old enough for his first two-wheel bicycle. Language plays its part in these gradations as well; the child is told he is too old to cry or too young to have some object he wants. *In some situations his age status is negotiable*: He may persuade his parents that he is old enough to go to the movies alone or old enough to have a shotgun. The negotiation of age status as an interactive process between parents and children has not received much study.

All these progressions lead the child toward maturity, a concept that has relevance both biologically and sociologically. Indeed, one of the important considerations for an understanding of socialization is that biological maturation usually presents a challenge to society or its agents. The child who becomes able to walk wants to walk in places that are "off limits" (for example, on furniture or in mud puddles) and therefore evokes negative sanctions. In similar fashion, other aspects of biological maturation, from eating to sexuality, present a challenge to society and its agencies and a challenge also to the growing child's own self. With each new step in biological maturation, the child feels ready to do things that once were done for him or wants to do things that his role models do, whether or not they feel he is ready. The child says "Let me do it" when the adult would rather do it more quickly himself or judges that the action is one the child should not yet do at all, even slowly—as when a three-year-old wants to use a sharp knife or carry something too heavy for him. Thus, from one perspective, socialization can be regarded as the process through which man's biological potentialities are brought into relationship with society: They are developed and transformed through time and made social.

No writer has achieved a more comprehensive view of this process than Erik Erikson.[26] In a sweeping look at the whole life cycle, he has proposed that it can be divided into eight stages, each of which presents the person with a basic socialization issue or dilemma. The manner in which each issue is resolved will shape the child's social participation as well as his individual happiness.

1. The first issue facing the helpless newborn is that of *trust versus distrust*. The emotional attachment to the mother is crucial in determining how this issue is resolved. From this standpoint, the first social achievement of the infant is his ability to let the mother out of sight without becoming anxious or enraged. This is possible when the mother has become "an inner certainty as well as an outer predictability."

2. The second year of life is marked by rapid gains in muscular maturation, visual and auditory discrimination, and verbalization. All of these give the child the possibility of greater control over his own actions, and he begins to experience a

sense of autonomous will. At this time, during which he is often also expected to gain bowel control, he is subjected to closer scrutiny. The issue posed by this level of development, according to Erikson, is that of *autonomy versus shame and doubt.* If the child is subjected to too much parental control, his sense of his smallness becomes overwhelming and he becomes vulnerable to shame or doubt about his ability to be self-directing.

3. In the next stage, about the third year of life, the child has mastered walking and is able to move about freely. His language capacity "becomes perfected to the point where he understands and can ask incessantly about innumerable things, often hearing just enough to misunderstand them thoroughly." His capacities for both language and locomotion enable him to imagine actions and roles that may frighten him. Thus is posed for him an issue of a *sense of initiative versus guilt.* The child explores and gets into things, both verbally and in action. His sense of rivalry with others is heightened. He also becomes aware of sex differences. Successful passage through this stage enables the child to feel that his own purposes have validity, that it is all right for him to move on his own toward things that seem interesting. If he is made to feel too frightened by his initiatives, he develops too stringent a conscience, dominated by a sense of guilt.

4. The next stage, extending over a period of several years, which Erikson calls the school age, is marked not so much by distinctive biological changes as by a more firmly modulated emotionality. (Schachtel's conventionalization of memory is proceeding at this time.) Children are ready to learn; they form attachments to teachers and parents of other children; they are interested in people practicing occupations that they can grasp—policemen, plumbers, garbagemen, and pilots, for example. They are also capable of fuller cooperation with others (Mead's game stage). There is growing acquaintance with the objects and practices of the society's technology. The issue presented by this developmental stage is called by

Erikson *industry versus inferiority.* Successful development through this stage gives the child a sense of his ability to work at tasks, both individually and in cooperation with others. If things do not go well, the child develops a sense of inferiority. This can come about in various ways:

> . . . the child may still want his mommy more than knowledge; he may still prefer to be the baby at home rather than the big child in school; he still compares himself with his father, and the comparison arouses a sense of guilt as well as a sense of inferiority. Family life may not have prepared him for school life, or school life may fail to sustain the promises of earlier stages in that nothing that he has learned to do well so far seems to count with his fellows or his teacher. . . . It is at this point that wider society becomes significant to the child by admitting him to roles preparatory to the actuality of technology and economy. Where he finds out immediately, however, that the color of his skin or the background of his parents rather than his wish and will to learn are the factors that decide his worth as a pupil or apprentice, the human propensity for feeling unworthy may be fatefully aggravated . . .[27]

5. The next period, adolescence, is the crucial period in Erikson's analysis of socialization. The period is initiated by puberty and is marked both by sexual maturation and by rapid growth in height and weight leading to the attainment of adult size. These changes set the basic task for the developing person: He must begin to find his own specific place in society. This is a period in which the person must work out for himself some integration of role models, values, norms, beliefs, emotional feelings. The issue of this period is that of *identity versus role diffusion.* Successful resolution of this issue results in the person's having a coherent sense of himself and his relationship to society. The person who is not able to utilize this period—and adolescence becomes ever more extended in our society, although we may now be entering a period of contraction—to find and establish a coherent sense of identity may be unable to find adult statuses and roles that are both personally satisfying and socially acceptable. He may be unable to settle upon an

occupation and generally unable to find a worthwhile way of life. Such socialization failures may be induced by socialization agencies that do not give adequate scope to diversity: "Youth after youth, bewildered by the incapacity to assume a role forced on him by the inexorable standardization of American adolescence, runs away in one form or another, dropping out of school, leaving jobs, staying out all night, or withdrawing into bizarre and inaccessible moods."[28]

The remaining three stages of the life cycle in Erikson's scheme go beyond the major concerns of this book. For the sake of completeness, we mention them briefly.

6. As people emerge from their identity struggles, they face the issue of *intimacy versus isolation.* This involves the ability to enter into relationships which in some sense involve self-abandon within a framework of trust: love, friendship, erotic encounters, experiences of joint inspiration.

7. The biological capability for parenthood does not necessarily lead to parenthood as a satisfying social role. The issue of this mature adult stage is *generativity versus stagnation,* generativity being "primarily the interest in establishing and guiding the next generation or whatever in a given case may become the absorbing object of a parental kind of responsibility."[29] Thus, Erikson does not mean that stagnation results from not being a parent in the literal sense. Rather, he means that the adult stagnates if he is not in *some* kind of role that involves fostering development, whether of a business or scientific research or a garden. (Indeed, sociologist Alice Rossi argues that parenthood in the literal sense —or at least motherhood—is an inappropriate role for many women and that American culture presses many women into maternity who are not very maternal and perhaps should not become mothers.[30])

8. The process of aging confronts the person with the issue of what kind of life he has lived, the issue of *integrity versus despair.* Integrity in this sense means a sense of wholeness:

. . . an emotional integration faithful to the image-bearers of the past. . . . the acceptance of one's one and only life cycle and of the people who have become significant to it as something that had to be and that, by necessity, permitted of no substitutions. It thus means a new and different love of one's parents, free of the wish that they should have been different, and an acceptance of the fact that one's life is one's own responsibility. It is a sense of comradeship with men and women of distant times and of different pursuits who have created orders and objects and sayings conveying human dignity and love.[31]

Erikson is the only modern social science theorist who has attempted a unified analysis of socialization through the entire life cycle from birth to death. For this reason his analysis is helpful in thinking about some of the complexities of this topic. Two issues concerning time have come to be recognized as troublesome: First, to what extent, if at all, does early socialization affect adult social behavior? Erikson views socialization as a cumulative process in which the resolution of the central issue at one stage affects the resolution of the issues presented by succeeding stages. He does not make any simple claim that the mother's treatment of her infant in the first year of life determines what kind of social being her child will be when adult. Rather, he is saying that the child's socialization in any one stage generates certain expectations, which the child brings with him into new socialization settings. The socializing agents in the new settings have their own expectations, which they direct toward the child. These agents become new role models that the child adds to those he already has. The child, then, has the task of creating some internal order for himself out of the expectations of the various socializing agents. The task is made easier, of course, when the expectations are similar, but as we pointed out early in this chapter, every child encounters some divergence of expectations.

The second question involves the relation of life-cycle time to historical time: How can parents (and other socializing agents) prepare their children to be adults in a society that will be very different when the children reach adulthood? The

answer to this question is not simple—and is far from completely available. But certain things can be said. One is that
social change is sometimes so great that socialization has in
fact not fitted children for the changed conditions. Erikson,
for example, describes the identity problems and social disorganization of Sioux Indians in North Dakota, who were still
being socialized to the values, skills, and way of life relevant
to hunting buffalo although all buffalo had been wiped out
decades earlier.[32]

Yet, clearly, in many situations adults do function in a
society that makes available statuses and roles that did not
exist when those adults were children. One explanation,
offered by Albert J. Reiss, is that early values learned in the
family setting are not internalized; the individual's behavior
changes as he moves from setting to setting and encounters
different values. To illustrate this, Reiss points out that the
same individual was able to function successfully in Germany
under the Weimer Republic, the Nazi regime, and the postwar
democratic political system.[33] But although it is true that the
same individual might have, under successive regimes, filled
different roles for which he had not been specifically prepared, the argument given by Reiss does not deal with the
possibility that certain kinds of early socialization may prepare a child to function adequately under successive drastic
change. For example, if the prime value inculcated in the Ger-
man child had been obedience to whatever authority held
effective sway, he might in this way have been socialized to
change roles in later life as the political institutions changed.

The relationship between socialization and social change
is one of the most intricate, and it is not settled either by
Reiss's argument or our objection to it. Perhaps Erikson again
best captures the intricacy of the problem:

... each generation of youth must find an identity consonant
with ideological promise in the perceptible historical process.
But in youth the tables of childhood dependence begin slowly
to turn: no longer is it merely for the old to teach the young the

meaning of life. It is the young who, by their responses and actions, tell the old whether life as represented to them has some vital promise, and it is the young who carry in them the power to confirm those who confirm them, to renew and regenerate, to disavow what is rotten, to reform and rebel.[34]

Some of the various ways in which time and conceptions of time affect socialization are illustrated in the following chapter.

4 Socialization and Subcultural Patterns

Any society that is large includes within it many different ways of life. To be sure, there are also important elements shared in common. Thus, in North America, for example, clothes, foods, tools, advertisements, kitchen appliances, drugstore displays, automobiles, popular sports, and many other elements are widely shared. Indeed, these elements are shared not only across two North American societies—Canadian and American—but in varying degrees across many others as well. But there are differences in emphasis which societies give even to these common elements. For example, the United States has accepted—or embraced—the automobile and given it far greater value than have other industrial societies. This shows up in several ways. None of the other societies that make extensive use of automobiles—Canada, Britain, France, Germany, and so forth—has so thoroughly subordinated rail transportation to the automobile as has the United States. Nor have these other societies been as willing to tear down buildings and clear land in the downtown areas of their cities for parking lots and garages. In short, although the automobile is used and valued in many societies, it receives greater emphasis in the United States than elsewhere and is more influential in affecting various kinds of social and political decisions.

The above examples illustrate a concept of great importance for socialization, the concept of *culture*. This concept originates in anthropology but has proved extremely useful in all the social sciences. Like all such concepts that try to capture a complex reality, it has been variously defined and interpreted. But the following definition would receive wide acceptance among anthropologists and sociologists and is suitable for our purposes: *A culture is a way of life developed by a people in adaptation to the physical and social circumstances in which they find themselves. It tends to be passed on from generation to generation, but it changes as circumstances change. It includes some elements that are highly valued by the people themselves and other elements that are accepted as necessary or "realistic" adaptations but are not especially valued.*

A tricky problem is presented by the terms *a culture* and *a people*. The fact is, as Margaret Mead points out, that these terms are somewhat elastic and apply to units of different scope, depending upon what one is trying to understand:

After deciding what larger unit we wish to refer to . . . then smaller observations are considered in terms of the regularities which have been identified for the whole. The term *cultural regularities* includes the way in which the versions of the culture found in different classes, regions, or occupations are systematically related to one another. So a member of the French bourgeoisie who is also a Protestant will manifest behavior which is French, which has certain peculiarities in common with the French bourgeois, and still others in common with his province, and others in common with his generation, etc. . . . when we are making a cultural analysis, we are interested in identifying those characteristics—including, if not specifying, the possibilities of variation by class, region, religion, etc.— which can be attributed to sharing in the tradition of the larger group, whether that group be nation, tribe, province, or some

even larger unit with a common tradition, such as the culture
of an area like Southeast Asia.[1]

The question of what unit a culture refers to has assumed
considerable importance in recent years for understanding
differences in socialization. Does the child growing up in an
isolated and poor rural hamlet in Kentucky have the same
culture as a child growing up in the middle of New York,
Chicago, or Houston? Does the child growing up in the slum
have the same culture as the child growing up in the affluent
suburb? The easiest answer to both questions is "No." The
visible differences are so great that it has become common
to insist that the children in these different settings are in
fact being socialized into different cultures. Closer examination suggests, however, that some cultural similarities are
simply less visible than the differences and that the differences are more likely to be necessary adaptations to circumstances than differences in values.[2] As an example, let
us take the value of career success. There is no question that
career success is a more dominant concern in some segments of society than in others. There are segments of American society, which we shall discuss shortly, in which men
have no evident interest in career success, contrasted with
others in which careers seem all important. It was fashionable at one time to regard the lack of interest in a career as
evidence of a value difference. Closer examination has shown,
however, that these men are not unmindful of the value
society places on a man's occupation. They have, however, for
reasons that lie largely beyond their control, lost all possibility for success or even a job. They share in the value that
others hold, but the value has lost meaning for their own
day-to-day lives because there seems to be no way in which
they can implement it.

This complex relationship of being both a part of a large
society yet in some ways marked off from it, participating in
a larger culture yet having a distinctive version of it, is

expressed in the terms *subsociety* and *subculture*. Charles Valentine emphasizes both the distinctiveness of subcultures and their interplay with the larger culture:

It is perhaps reasonable to assume that any subsociety may have a configuration of more or less distinguishable lifeways of its own. This configuration constitutes a subculture that is distinct from the total culture of the whole society in a . . . special and limited sense. The wider sociocultural system has its own coherence to which subsocieties and subcultures contribute even with their distinctiveness.[3]

What is the importance of subcultures for socialization? First, a child is socialized into a particular subculture, not into a culture as a whole. This means that initially a child learns not the ways of his society but the ways of a particular segment of it. He develops outlooks and assumptions that are not necessarily shared by those outside that segment. If he spends his entire lifetime associating only with those who share the same subculture, he may have difficulty understanding the thoughts, actions, and situations of those from other subcultures. The point may be illustrated with a hypothetical example. We might imagine a child in comfortable circumstances meeting a very poor child and asking him "How much allowance do you get?"—not realizing that in some parts of society children do not receive a weekly allowance. This is an example of a situation that affects all children in their early socialization but which most eventually leave behind as their experience widens: The things that are believed, valued, and done in one's own way of life lead to the implicit question "Doesn't everyone?"

A child's encounter with a different subculture can also take the reverse form. Instead of the revelation "I didn't know that everyone doesn't do what I do," the child may have an experience which takes the form "I didn't know other people do that." Thus, a young black woman whose mother cooked for a white family reports a childhood discovery:

Sometimes Mama would bring us the white family's leftovers. It was the best food I had ever eaten. That was when I discovered white folks ate different from us. They had all kinds of different food with meat and all. We always had just beans and bread.[4]

A child's "emergence" from his own subculture into an awareness of diversity may come early or late in life, and for some living in isolated and homogeneous communities it may never come at all.

Of course, with increasing urbanization, mobility, and education, a smaller and smaller proportion of children grows up so completely insulated within a subculture as to be unacquainted with other ways of living in the same society. Even the very small towns come under the influence of urbanization and its divergent ways.[5] These changes mean that more and more children are learning at some point in the course of their socialization that the answer to the question "Doesn't everyone?" is "No, everyone doesn't." Everyone does not belong to a country club; everyone does not go to church every Sunday; everyone does not live in a neighborhood of crowded apartments; everyone does not believe that the most important thing is to get a good job that leads to advancement and a house in a nice suburb; everyone does not live in decaying wooden houses in muddy hollows.

The general implication of the fact that socialization starts within a particular subculture is that *every* child's socialization in some measure *limits his ability to function in the larger society*. The values, beliefs, assumptions, and ways of life that come to be "second nature" to him make it difficult for him to function effectively in some kinds of social situations involving persons who have been socialized in other subcultures. The limiting effects of socialization are currently receiving considerable attention in the United States and indeed have become a matter of political conflict. On the one hand it is stated that lower-class children are socialized in such a way that they do not know how to function in a middle-class society. More recently, on the other hand, the contrary is also asserted: Middle-class people are so "locked in" by their values and norms that they do not understand the different subculture of lower-class people. This issue finds its most intense expression between black people and white people; the long held belief on the part of many whites that blacks cannot acquire many necessary kinds of competence because of their inferior way of life finds its answer today in a growing insistence by blacks that the socialization of whites renders them incompetent to meet the needs of blacks and to serve as socializing agents for black children. These bitter problems are but the latest form of what early sociologist William Graham Sumner saw many years ago as a universal social characteristic, which he named *ethnocentrism*: "Each group thinks its own folkways the only right ones. . . . Ethnocentrism leads a people to exaggerate and intensify everything in their own folkways which is peculiar and which differentiates them from others."[6] As Shibutani and Kwan have recently noted, ethnocentrism is one version of "trained incapacity"; it limits social competence.[7]

Although all cultures and subcultures necessarily generate some measure of ethnocentrism, some do so more than others. Isolation from other subcultures intensifies ethnocentrism, but so also do conflict and discrimination. Ethnocentrism is, in principle, modifiable, and many programs designed for its reduction are carried out by agencies concerned with human relations. Many social scientists go so far as to affirm that all socialization outcomes that limit social competence are modifiable by appropriate action programs.[8]

The importance of subcultures for socialization can be further appreciated by reference to concepts introduced earlier:

1. A person's *status* in society is partly determined by the subculture in which he participates.
2. A child's earliest *role models* are drawn from his own subculture, although by the time he reaches school age

he may already have encountered some role models from outside it.

3. Since a child's *self* is formed in large part by taking the role of others, and since his earliest significant others tend to be from his own subculture, the child's self has an anchor in a particular subculture.

Subcultures are based on different types of social differentiation. In the remainder of this chapter, we shall consider three of particular importance—social class, ethnic group, and community of residence—and ask how each of these affects socialization. In Chapter 5 we shall consider the relationship between subcultures and the major agencies of socialization.

Social Class

Although social class is variously defined in social science literature, virtually all social scientists recognize the existence of socioeconomic strata in our society and acknowledge that different groups possess unequal amounts of wealth, influence, prestige, and "life chances." Such inequalities have consequences and ramifications that sociologists feel justified in interpreting as aspects of social class. Some Americans may deny the existence of social classes, because social classes involve rankings of categories of people and because of the belief that "every man is just as good as any other." But in practice even these people often make use of terms that differentially evaluate categories of people and their ways of life: terms such as "decent people," "jet set," "beatniks," "lazy no-goods," "workingmen," "hippies," and even "middle class" and "lower class."

Children can become aware of social class differences even at elementary school age if they have any opportunity to mingle with children of more than one social class. Thus, one investigator, in a study of a New England industrial town, reports that children between the fourth and sixth grades begin to distinguish such symbols of social class as evening dress and riding horseback clothed in a riding habit; and by the eighth grade, adult stereotypes of social class are quite generally known.[9] Another sociologist, studying children aged ten to twelve in "Jonesville," a city in the Midwest, found that children of the upper-middle class were generally judged by their classmates to be better looking and fairer playing than lower-class children, differences that were understandable only in terms of the social class positions of the children themselves.[10]

Social Class As a Way of Life

From the point of view of socialization, perhaps the most important aspect of social stratification is a group's "way of life" or subculture. There are many ways of life associated with social class, ranging from a very small "upper upper" class with its genealogy, mansions, servants, yachts, debutantes, and private school education down to the déclassé. For purposes of illustration and contrast, in this section we shall focus on socialization in two class groups—one, the so-called upper-middle class, the other generally designated the lower class.

Perhaps the readiest means of identifying a person's social class membership is by his occupation. The upper-middle class consists primarily of families whose breadwinners are relatively affluent (though not wealthy) professionals and businessmen. In the lower class the breadwinner is generally an unskilled laborer who works irregularly. In these days, when unskilled labor is increasingly replaced by machines, it also includes men (and their families) who, having no skill, may be chronically unemployed. The lower class also includes families, often without a male head, whose income derives largely from public assistance. Thus, not the least important fact about the lower class is that it is poor, but the differences between it and the upper-middle class are not simply income and what it buys. Social classes are ways of life and therefore socialization environments for the children born into them. At the same time, as we have observed, the lines between particular subcultures are not always clearly drawn. This is particularly true with regard to values. There has been some controversy in recent years as to whether all social classes in a society are oriented to the same or different values. Considerable light on this controversy has been cast by Hyman Rodman whose analysis of several research studies leads him to conclude that the lower class develops a "value stretch." As he puts it, "The lower class value stretch refers to the wider range of values and the lower degree of commitment to these values to be found within the lower class."[11] The implications of this will be discussed in this and the following chapters.

Upper-Middle-Class Subculture

Upper-middle-class men generally are greatly concerned with developing successful careers, whether as independent professionals or as salaried executives working in large organizations. This means that they are oriented to the future and look to expanding responsibilities, prestige, and income —at least until that time in life when each man recognizes that he has attained his maximum. One of the important distinguishing characteristics of middle-class as compared with lower-class occupations is that they require a greater degree of self-direction.[12] To carry on such an occupation with even a moderate amount of success requires a certain kind of self: a belief in one's ability to face and solve problems and to make judgments and decisions. Confidence that one's own actions make a difference in how things turn out is also required. Although there are uncertainties, anxieties, and disappointments in pursuing a career, and many men fall short of "making it" as they had hoped, the upper-middle-class man's life is dominated by a concern with career and future. As he pursues these goals, he is managing himself and his situation.

His wife is also likely to think of herself as an effective, "doing" sort of person. She may or may not be employed, but in either case she manages a busy schedule of activities. Often she is involved in some kind of volunteer charity. The outspoken wife of one professional man compares herself with her husband in these terms: "We both handle people the same; we expect top work from employees. We have pretty high standards, but we're fair. It's all stated clearly, few words minced, and that's how it's going to be and we stay with it."[13]

The accomplishments of the upper-middle-class bread-winner generally give him an income that enables his family to live at a high level of material comfort. The family residence is likely to be substantial, though not palatial, and it is well stocked with a wide range of consumer goods, some of which are likely to be rather costly. The dwelling usually is large enough for each child to have a room of his own; when this is not the case, the family is likely to look forward to the time when its income will increase sufficiently for this standard to be attained. Privacy is a value, and it is felt that even children require privacy. Privacy in this form costs money, and the upper-middle-class family generally has enough money, sooner or later, to buy it.

The upper-middle-class way of life usually involves its members in a variety of institutions outside the family. The father's occupation, for example, may require him to be in contact with many organizations in addition to the one that employs him. If he is a businessman, he is involved in buying and selling relationships with people in other firms. If he is a professional, he is associated with hospitals or courts or universities or government agencies, where he meets other men with whom he collaborates or whom he helps, persuades, or teaches, as the case may be. He is, to use a somewhat quaint expression, "a man of affairs." (Sex roles have not yet changed sufficiently to allow us to speak of "a woman of affairs" in quite the same sense.)

In addition to occupational contacts with many organizations, the man and his wife are likely to have roles in numerous other formal organizations—associations of business or professional men (medical societies, law groups, chambers of commerce, and so on), church groups, country clubs or swimming clubs, and perhaps some civic betterment association. In addition to activities in these formal organizations, there is likely to be considerable entertaining at home, largely arranged by the wife, as well as such out-of-home entertainment as dining in good restaurants and attending the theater, concerts, and the like.

Children growing up in this class also begin early to have a diversified social participation, much of it sponsored and controlled by adults. They are likely to belong to one or more such organizations as the Boy Scouts, the Girl Scouts, athletic teams, church and synagogue groups, camera clubs, and community center groups. The schools sponsor many extracurricular activities; in a study of an upper-middle-class suburb, one school principal reported that there were forty-two extracurricular organizations in his school.[14] In addition, children go away to summer camp and, during the school year, may take lessons in music, dancing, swimming, skiing, or tennis. It is part of the value system of this class, to quote one research report, that

Parents and adult leaders of children's associations expect the cooperation and gratitude of the child "for all that is being done for him." Such associations should, in adult eyes, satisfy all the child's recreational needs. Adult reaction to the child-centered, child-controlled associations which do develop outside the orbit of adult control is one of marked suspicion and some anger, the elders' direct response to a rejection of their well-meant efforts.[15]

Since the upper-middle class is increasingly concentrated in suburbs (although not all suburbs are upper-middle class or even middle-class), the child's social participation in these varied activities often involves his being driven from one location to another—not by an employed chauffeur but mostly by his mother, on weekends perhaps by his father, and sometimes by friends or neighbors through the medium of "car pools" which are formed by several parents whose children are engaged in similar activities. This is one device among many by which upper-middle-class parents guide and keep tabs on their children's way of life.

The upper-middle class is intently focused on its children's future and directs a great deal of effort to attempting to prepare children for it. At the same time, upper-middle class people generally expect that their children's future will be quite different from their own current adulthood, although they do not know in what ways it will differ. Partly for this reason, self-direction receives great emphasis as a value in the upper-middle class. This emphasis derives not only from the anticipation of the future but also, as Melvin J. Kohn has shown, from the father's current position. Kohn analyzes the situation as follows: Values are products of life conditions. While many such conditions affect values, one that is particularly salient is the general structure of the man's work. Upper-middle-class occupations are distinguished from working-class occupations in that the former involve more self-direction and self-reliance, less close supervision, and—with certain exceptions—greater involvement with ideas than with things. The reverse is generally true for working-class occupations, although again there are exceptions. Corresponding to this social class difference in occupations, Kohn finds a difference in emphasis on values between these two classes. Middle-class people value both obedience and self-direction in their children but place greater emphasis on the latter. Working-class people, in contrast, place much greater emphasis on obedience and are less concerned with self-direction. This difference was found to hold not only in the United States but also in Turin, an industrial city in Italy, as well.[16] Related to this is a social class difference in disciplining children: Middle-class parents are more concerned with the intent of a child's acts, whereas working- and lower-class parents are more concerned with overt consequences of what children do. Middle-class parents are anxious that their children internalize standards; working-class parents are anxious that their children learn to behave respectably.[17] (Kohn's studies have dealt with the stable working class rather than with the lower class as defined above. We refer to his comparisons here because they help to clarify the value emphasis in the upper-middle class.)

Significant social class differences also exist in the use of language. As we pointed out in Chapter 3, language is one of the important ways—some sociologists believe the most important—in which social reality is organized. Insofar as social classes use language differently they are organizing their realities differently. Basil Bernstein suggests that one of the most significant relationships between social class and language is that in the upper-middle class language becomes the object of special attention and elaboration. The structure and syntax of middle-class speech are particularly complex and make possible a more subtle and complex grasp of reality than is the case in the lower class. Bernstein illustrates with a homely example, a middle-class mother saying to her child, "I'd rather you made less noise, dear." The middle-class child has learned to interpret "rather" and "less" as imperative cues for his response. Bernstein believes that the lower-class child does not have available this kind of sentence structure and would have to translate the foregoing sentence into a form that he knows from his own experience—"Shut up!"[18] Another study reports that middle-class mothers use many more words than do lower-class mothers in talking to their children, that more of the words are abstract, and that the sentences are longer and more complex.[19]

Bernstein's argument about language parallels Kohn's on values: Both language styles and values arise as adaptations to class-based situations. Upper-middle-class values and language style both reflect the class's complex involvement in organizations and the requirements for self-reliance in making judgments about abstract matters.

The career and future orientation of the upper-middle class and the great emphasis on developing self-direction in its children have been interpreted to mean that the socialization of middle-class children, from infancy through college and graduate school, is characterized by their deferring basic gratifications in order to attain future goals. This deferred gratification pattern, as it has been called, includes such diverse aspects as the postponement of being employed and independent in order to attain a more elaborate education, saving money rather than spending it freely as the spirit moves, controlling aggressive impulses and staying out of fights, and avoiding sexual intercourse until one is married and "settled."[20] When the concept "deferred gratification pattern" was first introduced into the literature, few questioned its relevance.

Contemporary efforts to gain fuller understanding of the working class and lower class, partly in order to understand what really differentiates them from the middle class, have led to some challenge of the validity of the deferred gratification pattern. Thus, Miller and Riessman ask:

Is it really true today in the prosperous middle class youth culture of the United States that most middle class youth are deferring gratification when they go to college? More likely, many look upon it in anticipation and retrospect as coming closest in their total experiences to the realization of gratifications. Frequently, it seems that the working class is compared with an inner-directed, economically marginal middle class of yore than with an "acting-out," "other-directed," "affluent" middle class of today. The shifts in the middle class, murky as they are, make it especially difficult and dubious to use it as a yardstick for elucidating (and frequently evaluating) working class life.[21]

There is undoubtedly some justice in this challenge. To picture socialization of the middle-class child as being focused on austerity, asceticism, and self-restraint is to disregard the evidence that the American middle class allows more pleasure in the socialization of its children than was formerly true. However, it is doubtful that the earlier picture is now completely outdated. Miller and Riessman comment only on the college years, not on the childhood years of middle-class socialization. It seems likely that despite the greater indulgence of upper-middle-class children today as compared with the past, they nevertheless remain more closely supervised and more intensively guided toward adult roles than the children of the lower class or even the stable working class. In this same vein, though the college years may be gratifying, it remains nonetheless true that preparation for an upper-middle-class occupation requires sustained application and more or less rigorous self-discipline. Whether deferral of gratification is the most significant feature of this process may be questionable. But at the very least it would seem that the upper-middle-class child is more insistently reminded of his future and required to be more prudent in his actions. Although it is more than a quarter of a century since Allison Davis noted that the pressures on the upper-middle-class child generate in him an "adaptive" or "socialized anxiety," it is doubtful that his observations have become altogether outdated by recent social changes.[22] Indeed, it seems evident that the *counter-culture*, including the wide popularity of drug taking and the liberation of sexual expression among middle-class youth, is partly an effort to escape from the stringent pressures of upper-middle-class socialization (although these phenomena have other causes as well).

Lower-Class Subculture

The term *lower class* has two principal meanings. Its more neutral meaning denotes those in a society who have the least of the benefits a society distributes: income, influence, education, prestige, and the many additional benefits such as good housing and secure and possibly satisfying employment that follow from these. The term has additional connotations, particularly to many middle-class people: It is used to refer unfavorably to the way of life followed by people so situated. Thus, *lower class* implies ignorance; instability of employment and family life; "premature" initiation of heterosexual activity and subsequent promiscuity; "low standards" of personal grooming, housekeeping, and language usage—in short, a wide array of behavior that is unacceptable to middle-class people. These judgmental connotations make it difficult for middle-class people to consider lower-class life with detachment and therefore raise some questions about continued use of the label. We use the term of course in its first meaning.

Lower-class subculture is not strongly oriented toward the future—because lower-class people are intensively preoccupied with problems of survival in the present. Albert K. Cohen and Harold M. Hodges, in their study of lower-class life on the San Francisco Peninsula, identify four main aspects of the lower-class person's life situation:[23]

1. *Deprivation.* Lower-class people feel deprived. They have inadequate resources compared with their felt needs and levels of aspiration. Although it is possible to feel deprived at any level of life, lower-class people feel more chronically deprived of more things than do people at other class levels. These include not only income and what it can buy but also such valued goals as education, satisfying work, happy marriage, and enjoyment of life.

2. *Insecurity.* Lower-class life is especially unpredictable, entailing high vulnerability to sickness, injury, disability, death, and entanglements with the law. And when these misfortunes occur, there are fewer resources to deal with them. People have neither the funds nor the necessary skills, knowledge, and access to institutions that can help.

3. *Simplification of the experience world.* Lower-class people move in a more narrowly defined world, both geographically and socially, than do people of other classes. They have experienced a relatively limited range of objects and situations and have limited perspectives from which to define, classify, and evaluate their experiences.

4. *Powerlessness.* The lower-class adult has little "leverage" in society. His relatively low level of skill makes him easily replaceable in employment; "he has the least access to and control over strategically important information." In general, he feels little ability to influence the course of his own life. Not only have lower-class people experienced little previous success in shaping their own lives, they expect little in the future. Their pessimism is summarized by Cohen and Hodges:

"A body just can't take nothing for granted; you just have to live from day to day and hope the sun will shine tomorrow." No theme more consistently runs through the pattern of the LL's [lower-class person's] responses and distinguishes him from the others. In his view, nothing is certain; in all probability, however, things will turn out badly as they generally have in the past.[24]

Furthermore, lower-class people know that they are "at the bottom of the heap" and looked down upon by people more favorably situated in society. Thus, they face the problem of evolving a way of life that will, insofar as possible, reduce insecurity and serve as a defense against moral criticism. One way in which this is done is to maintain a network of relationships with people situated similarly to themselves, primarily neighbors and kin. In this way they are able to call upon others in time of need. Another aspect of this way of life is to place heavy reliance on fate, chance, or luck; belief in such factors as causes of their destiny helps to relieve the sense of failure. Yet these and other adaptations to a harsh reality do not always eliminate despair and a sense of ineffectiveness. Eleanor Pavenstadt describes what she saw in lower-class homes that she studied:

The outstanding characteristic . . . was that activities were impulse-determined; consistency was totally absent. The mother might stay in bed until noon while the children were kept in bed as well or ran around unsupervised. Another time she might decide to get them up and give them breakfast at 6, have them washed and dressed and the apartment picked up by 8:30. Or the children might get their breakfast from the neighbors . . . These mothers always dressed their children. . . . None of the children owned anything; a recent gift might be taken away by another sibling without anyone's intervening. The parents often failed to discriminate between the children: a parent, incensed by the behavior of one child, was seen dealing a blow to another child who was close by. Communications by words hardly existed. . . .[25]

This quotation emphasizes the disorganization of lower-class home life. Yet closer reading indicates some effort, even if only episodic, to live up to norms that are shared by the wider society—for example, washing and dressing the children, picking up the apartment. Inconsistency of behavior in the lower class, including inconsistency in socialization of its children, has been one of its most readily recognizable aspects since sociologists began studying differences in the ways of life of the different social classes. More recent observations and analyses have directed our attention to the fact that the lower-class subculture includes values and norms that are central to middle-class culture but which often cannot be sustained under the conditions of lower-class life. The lower-class person's actions oscillate between conformity to values and to countervailing circumstances.

Moreover, some of the characteristics that were often thought to be distinctive of lower-class culture are now more fully understood not simply as "their way" but as adaptations to deprivation. Thus, Cohen and Hodges, as have others, note that "toughness" is an important quality in lower-class life. This includes a "dog-eat-dog" ideology; pride in the ability to "take it"; and a general posture of assertiveness, a "don't-push-me-around" touchiness. But while toughness sometimes manifests itself as belligerence, other observers have emphasized another aspect, the capacity to endure hardship. One mother explains why she kept her children home from school:

There was no food in the house and I didn't want them to have to go to school hungry and then come home hungry too. I felt that if I kept them home with me, at least when they cried and asked for a piece of bread, I would be with them to put my arms around them.[26]

The Middle Class and the Working Class

We have discussed upper-middle class and lower-class sub-cultures because, on the one hand, they are two quite contrasting socialization environments within the same society, yet, on the other hand, there are some important similarities between them. Between the upper-middle and the lower classes in the urban world are other strata, conveniently designated "working class" and "lower-middle class." The former includes skilled workers in manufacturing, trades, and service occupations (such as barbers), who are generally employed steadily and whose way of life is seen as stable both by themselves and by others. Very often they belong to labor unions and thus have some sense of being able to influence decisions that affect their own lives. The lower-middle class includes many kinds of white-collar workers—owners of small neighborhood stores, supervisory employees in large organizations, many salesmen. Working-class people today generally have graduated from high school; lower-middle-class people have often had some college and many have graduated. The reader interested in learning more about these subcultures is referred to the appropriate literature.[27]

Community of Residence

Our discussion of social class subcultures has been based on work carried out primarily in metropolitan areas and in small towns. We were not concerned with community of residence as a basis for differentiating subcultures, although the residential community is increasingly linked to social class. Thus, upper-middle-class people increasingly live in suburbs (although, to repeat, not all suburbs are upper-middle class). Lower-class people live in slums in the "inner city" areas of large cities and in run-down areas in small towns. To an important extent, then, analyzing a subculture from the standpoint of social class and from the standpoint of community of residence are simply two different approaches to the same task. We believe that the social class approach contributes fuller understanding (although not all sociologists would agree). Nevertheless, a community's history, geography, and economy do contribute to subcultural variation and, therefore, to socialization, particularly if the community is relatively isolated. Let us present a brief sketch of one subculture in a relatively isolated area.

The Subculture of a Depressed Area

We shall describe some aspects of the subculture of the Cumberland Plateau, a mountainous area consisting of nineteen counties in eastern Kentucky, as it has been portrayed by Harry M. Caudill.[28]

The Cumberland Plateau is an area of steep ridges and narrow, winding valleys, part of the Appalachian Mountains. It is inhabited by about half a million people, most of whom are descendants of English, Welsh, Irish, and Scottish pioneers who first settled the area long before the Declaration of Independence. The people who live in the area today are part of that backwoods group derogatorily referred to in other parts of the country as "hillbillies."

Families and neighbors were divided by the Civil War. Cousins, brothers, and even fathers and sons often took opposing sides. When the occupants of a mountain cabin learned that a relative had died in the war, they took revenge against the nearest available family whose members were sympathetic to the opposite side. A tradition of hatred and violence was established, and it developed into the ferocious Kentucky mountain feuds that lasted unchecked until 1915. "Thus the mountaineer came to inherit the hatreds of his father along with his name. . . . The mountaineers' hatreds became so many-layered, so deeply ingrained and so tenaciously remembered that they were subconscious, and as such they have, to a remarkable degree, been transmitted to his present-day descendants."[29] The transmission of hatreds of ancient origin is one illustration of the way in which historic events can shape the socialization process.

Between 1875 and 1910 the mountaineers lost most of their land to big-city entrepreneurs from the North and East. Being isolated from the rest of the country, they were unaware of the growing industrialization and consequently of the value of the timber and coal on their lands. Also, being illiterate and unsophisticated, many had not adequately registered and secured title to the land, some of which had been given as a veterans' benefit at the close of the Revolutionary War. Much of the land slipped from their hands either through acceptance of nominal payment or through court action.

Absentee-owned coal companies came to dominate the economy; the mountaineers were recruited to work in the newly developing mines. Since there were no towns in the region—the largest town was often the county seat with no more than 150 people—the companies built camps to house the miners. In many of them the housing was ramshackle, built of unseasoned lumber, so that in a few years the houses began to sag and sway. Miners were required to live in these company-owned houses, as a condition of employment, and to pay rent to their employer. Although the coal companies also built school buildings, the schools were inadequately financed because the companies were powerful enough to keep their taxes low. Since there was not enough money to pay qualified teachers, most left the area and were replaced by children of mountaineers; their training went no further than a semester or two at a state teachers college.

During the early years of the coal towns, some efforts were made by both companies and residents to keep them clean. This proved to be a losing battle as coal dust seeped into everything. The polluted atmosphere peeled paint from the walls and turned clothing yellowish gray. Despite best efforts, the communities turned "coal-camp gray." Caudill describes the effects on the housewife:

Many women fought the dirt-and-grime battle through the best years of their lives and surrendered to it only in old age, long after the Big Boom and the Great Depression were history.
. . . Realizing that the contest could not be won, they slowly capitulated to the unremitting clouds and allowed their homes to lose the sparkle and shine which had characterized the new towns. The spick-and-span gave way to the dull and disordered, and the women sat down on the front-porch swings and in chairs before the fireplaces and allowed the victorious enemy to run riot through the towns. There appeared the first symptoms of the vacuity, resignation and passivity which so marks the camp dwellers today, traits which could only deepen as the years brought new defeats and new tragedies.[30]

The boom period in coal mining ended in the late 1920s, and the economy of the area never really recovered, although there was a brief upsurge after World War II. One important factor was that coal mining became mechanized, so there were few jobs for men who knew no other skill but mining. By the end of 1957 more than half the people in some counties were regularly existing upon food supplied by government relief. Efforts of many men to find jobs in cities such as Cincinnati, Detroit, or Chicago were fruitless. Many younger people did succeed in leaving the area for jobs elsewhere, thus leaving the area depleted of energy and ability. The great unemployment and "the flight from the plateau of its hardier people" resulted, Caudill states, in "the growth of 'welfarism' on a scale unequaled elsewhere in North America and scarcely surpassed anywhere in the world."

One of the central features, if not indeed the dominant one, of this subculture at the present time is a sense of demoralization. Men over forty can find employment neither in the area nor elsewhere. Many of the homes are rotting and almost beyond repair. The area has one of the highest birth rates in the United States, and this, together with the extensive unemployment, leads to widespread, and often devious, efforts to become eligible for one or another program of public assistance. Children who manage to graduate from high school usually leave the area; by a year after graduation, no more than 4 or 5 percent of the graduates remain in their home counties. Some of the important consequences of this subculture for socialization are revealed in an interview with a fifty-six-year-old jobless miner:

I hain't got no education much and jist barely can write my name. After I lost my job in 1950 I went all over the country a-lookin' fer work. I finally found a job in a factory in Ohio a-puttin' televisions inside wooden crates. Well I worked for three years and managed to make enough money to keep my young-uns in school. Then they put in a machine that could crate them televisions a whole lot better than us men could and in a lot less time. Hit jist stapled them up in big card-board boxes. I got laid off again and I jist ain't never been able to find nothing else to do.

But I kept my young'uns in school anyway. I come back home here to the mountains and raised me a big garden ever' year and worked at anything I could find to do. I sold my old car fer seventy-five dollars and I sold all the land my daddy left me and spent the money on my children. They didn't have much to eat or wear, but they at least didn't miss no school. Well, finally last spring my oldest boy finished up high school and got his diploma. I managed to get twenty-five dollars together and give it to him and he went off to git him a job. He had good grades in school and I figured he'd get him a job easy. He went out to

California where he's got some kinfolks and went to a factory where they was hirin' men. The sign said all the work hands had to be under thirty-five years of age and be high-school graduates. Well, this company wouldn't recognize his diploma because it was from a Kentucky school. They said a high-school diploma from Kentucky, Arkansas, and Mississippi just showed a man had done about the same as ten years in school in any other state. But they agreed to give the boy a test to see how much he knowed and he failed it flatter than a flitter. They turned him down and he got a job workin' in a laundry. He jist barely makes enough money to pay his way but hit's better than settin' around back here.

I reckon they jist ain't no future fer people like us. Me and my wife ain't got nothin' and don't know nothin' hardly. We've spent everything we've got to try to learn our young-'uns something so they would have a better chance in the world, and now they don't know nothin' either![31]

This man's case is not atypical in the area. The interview suggests that the values in this subculture—at least with respect to preparing children for adult roles—are not very different from those of upper-middle-class subculture, although there are differences in many norms. The interview also indicates some of the ways in which even a relatively isolated subsociety is part of the larger society. And it brings out significant effects of economic conditions on a subculture and socialization into it. Stories of the relative success of some who have moved away and the view of the world offered by television provide some role models that are more diverse than those present locally and thus stimulate aspirations; but the resources actually operative in the subculture are insufficient to develop in the young more than a minimal competence to occupy adult roles in an industrial society. As Richard A. Ball points out in his analysis of Appalachian subculture, the young learn to expect defeat, and much of the culture can be understood as consisting of efforts to seek relief from insoluble problems.[32]

The effects of isolation on the socialization process are vividly brought out in a report from another part of Appalachia:

Mountain people are indeed reared in a society of the 'known,' a rural environment providing little stimulation or opportunity, and thus acquire neither the attitude of mind nor the few skills needed for meeting new and different situations. There are few broadening experiences available to them—few simple experiences like sitting with people you don't know on a bus, asking for change from a busdriver, doing business with strangers in stores or supermarkets, meeting and playing with strange children in the park. . . . Because mountain children are surrounded by a culture that contains only what is known, they are often extremely reluctant and afraid to attempt any unfamiliar experience.

For example, a group of men from our area were being housed in a YMCA in a city where the church was seeking to relocate them. One night a member of the group stopped in the lobby for a candy bar while the others went on up to their rooms. Following along afterwards, he entered the automatic elevator, which had always been operated by someone else in the group. Finding himself alone with the doors closed, he panicked. He yelled and screamed and beat on the sides of the elevator until someone on the outside punched the button, opening the doors for him. He was so shaken by this experience that the next day he boarded a bus for home. . . . Here was a young man in his early thirties who was so overwhelmed in this new situation that he could not handle his fear.[33]

Ethnic Groups

The population of North America derives from immigrants from many countries. Those whose families came several generations ago from northern Europe are now often thought of as "native" Americans; those whose families came more recently from such countries as Greece, Poland, Hungary, and Mexico are more often considered ethnic minorities.

The mass immigration of relatively uneducated southern and eastern Europeans to the United States was halted by legislation passed in the early 1920s, and relatively few immigrants of similar backgrounds have come since. In recent years, however, Mexicans and especially Puerto Ricans have arrived in large numbers. The Puerto Ricans, who are American citizens, number over 800,000 in the United States, of whom three-quarters live in New York City. Currently, then, for Puerto Ricans and many Mexicans, it is the first and second generations who are being socialized into American life; for the older immigrant groups, it is generally the third generation and beyond.

Of course, the largest minority group in the United States is not an immigrant group at all: the blacks, who have been in the country almost as long as the whites. (In 1790, when the first census was taken, Negroes made up 19.3 percent of the population.[34]) In defining the ethnic group, Shibutani and Kwan state that it "consists of those who conceive of themselves as being alike by virtue of their common ancestry, real or fictitious, and who are so regarded by others."[35] There can be little doubt that, despite their long residence in the country, blacks have been regarded by others as being alike by virtue of common ancestry. Today, increasingly, they so regard themselves, accepting the definition the larger society has thrust upon them and striving to change its meaning from one of derogation to one of pride.

An ethnic group typically has a subordinate status in the larger society of which it is a part. "In almost all instances of inter-ethnic contact, people of subordinate rank have sooner or later learned the ways of the dominant group. The concept of *acculturation* refers to the process of acquiring the culture of another ethnic group."[36] The adaptation of any ethnic group to American culture depends on various factors: how "different" the group feels itself to be or is regarded by others; the group's degree of cohesion; its particular skills and educational level; popular images of its native country and people; and, significantly, the economic, political, and social conditions prevailing in America at any given time. Thus, there are many variations between and within ethnic groups, but the process of socialization for immigrants and their descendants nevertheless presents certain characteristic patterns. The patterns are, of course, different among black Americans, who did not come as immigrants but were brought here as slaves, and among American Indians, who were here long before both the immigrants and the blacks arrived.

The child learns his ethnic status in the normal course of his development. His significant others serve as models for behavior and feelings associated with ethnic status, and, often in such questions as "Why am I Polish?" or "Why can't I have a Christmas tree?" he indicates his awareness of differences between himself and others.

Various studies indicate that minority-group children are aware of their distinct statuses by the time they are six or seven years old and often earlier, although they are too young to understand abstract aspects of status differentiations. In a study of four-year-old Negro and white children in New England, Mary Ellen Goodman found not only race awareness but race prejudice.[37] Compared with other children, minority-group children "show earlier and greater differentiation of their own group as well as more personal involvement in the group identification."[38]

In the following sections, we shall discuss socialization in the second and third generations, recognizing, of course, that the lines between generations are necessarily blurred.[39]

Socialization in the Second Generation

The child of the immigrant learns two cultures and two identities, those of his ethnic group and those of the national society. His ethnic culture and identity are learned through hearing stories of group experiences, idealizing group heroes, observing and sympathizing with family members in their interaction with fellow ethnics and with outsiders, and generally through participating in the group's way of life. He learns the culture, not in its "pure" form but as modified and practiced in the new country. In her study of Puerto Ricans, Elena Padilla writes:

The culture of the Puerto Ricans in New York cannot be characterized as "Puerto Rican" for it is not the same as

that of Puerto Ricans in Puerto Rico. . . . Even the Spanish
language spoken in New York differs from that of Puerto
Rico. . . . Many of these [words and phrases] are derived from
English and assimilated into the Spanish the migrants
brought with them.[40]

Outside of his immediate family and ethnic group, the
child experiences the new American society and culture
with their different customs, loyalties, and prejudices. The
aspects of the new world that are learned about from advertisements, movies, headlines, and department store displays
are likely to be characteristic of the country as a whole and
to contrast with aspects that characterize a limited local
setting. Immigrants who live in the lowest-rent neighborhoods often learn about America from a distinctly "slum
point of view."[41] The array of specialized institutions that
make up the urban Negro ghetto, to which many thousands
of rural Negroes have migrated in recent decades, is
described by Hylan Lewis:

Carry-out shops, laundromats, and record shops have recently
come to the ghetto in numbers. They join taverns, pool halls,
liquor stores, corner groceries, rooming houses, secondhand
stores, credit houses, pawn shops, industrial insurance
companies, and storefront churches as parts of a distinctive
complex of urban institutions that have undergone changes in
adapting to the effective wants, limited choices, and mixed
tastes of inner-city residents. Inner-city carry-out shops
serve many functions other than selling prepared food.
Among other things they may serve as informal communication
centers, forums, places to display and assess talents, and
staging areas for a wide range of activities, legal, illegal,
and extra-legal. And although they exist in the heart of the
city, they are like outpost institutions—gathering places
for outsiders in the center of the city.[42]

These are the institutions with which the lower-class urban
Negro child becomes familiar.

Perhaps the most important agency of socialization teaching the broader American culture is the school, although
television has perhaps acquired competing importance as
no earlier media did. Anthropologist Toshio Yatsushiro,

writing of the second-generation Japanese on the West Coast, says:

More than any other single force, the American school molded the character of the Nisei. . . . They responded eagerly to the relatively free and permissive school atmosphere which was in direct contrast to the rigid family life they led. They were able to interact rather freely with the members of the majority group, and in doing so assimilated . . . traits of the majority culture. Among other things, they were quick to pick up slang and cursing."[43]

That misunderstandings, frustrations, and conflicts develop between parents and children in such cases is not surprising. The parents, with their traditional set of values, are often dismayed at the behavior and attitudes of their children, and the latter, in turn, resent the ideas of their parents. The comment of a Mexican-American girl is representative of the experiences of children from many ethnic groups:

My mother and dad got too many old-fashioned ideas. She's from another country. I'm from America, and I'm not like her. With Mexican girls they want you to sit like *moscas muertas*, dead flies, like that. If you tell them what the teachers say, they say the teachers don't know. . . . I remember when me and my sister told my mother we wanted to dress neat and American they beat us and said no.[44]

In such cases, it is generally the immigrant parents, unable to draw on the broader culture and social system to support their position, who must try to make the major adaptation. In the terms of Erikson, in the quotation at the conclusion of Chapter 3, the children are not "confirming" their parents; the life which the parents hold out as correct does not represent a "vital promise" in the new environment, as the children see it. What is happening is that the children are *changing their reference groups.* A reference group is any group by whose standards one judges one's own behavior.[45] The parents and their ethnic group are no longer regarded as a suitable reference group. The children increasingly judge themselves by the standards of their American age-mates or peers, because, of course, they are being judged by them on the street and in school.

The child of the ethnic minority group has two statuses: an ethnic (Mexican, Italian, Japanese, or whatever) and an American status. A child, as a Greek, may be proud of his national heritage and religion; as an American he may be aware of his foreign-sounding name and his parents' strong accent. The child lives on the margins of two cultures, has loyalties to both, but is not completely participant in either. As Shibutani and Kwan observe:

Many of the problems confronting such individuals arise from their having to perform for two different and incongruous reference groups. Since contradictory demands are made upon them by the two audiences, they experience inner conflicts. When a man lives in two social worlds, each of which is a moral order, he cannot live up to all of his obligations. Where standards are inconsistent, he will be wrong in the eyes of one of the groups no matter what he does. He may be plagued by a sense of guilt even when he has done his very best. Some persons sometimes have difficulty developing a consistent self-conception. As Cooley pointed out, a man comes to conceive of himself as a particular kind of human being in response to the manner in which others treat him. But what happens to a man who looks simultaneously into two mirrors and sees sharply different images of himself?[46]

Developing a consistent self-conception or identity is, as we noted earlier, a task for every child, but it is accentuated for the child who is marginal to two cultures.

Socialization in the Third Generation

Most members of the third generation readily assimilate the major elements of American culture and their social class positions within it. That they no longer speak the language of the old country or follow traditional customs does not bother them. Nevertheless, the values of the past are not completely lost; they persist particularly in their orientation toward achievement and in their ethnic or religious identification.

In earlier generations new immigrants, often having come from rural peasant areas and without specialized training, began at the lowest socioeconomic rungs and "pushed up" those who had arrived before. The group that had been at the bottom moved up a notch when a new group began immigrating. For the grandchildren of immigrants, this progression in status no longer holds, for different ethnic groups have advanced at different rates. Some, by virtue of their traditions and socialization patterns, have absorbed more easily than others American values of mobility and achievement. For example, in comparing Jews and Italians in New Haven, Fred L. Strodtbeck reports that "Jews consistently have higher occupational status than the population at large, while, in contrast, Italians are consistently lower."[47]

The differences in achievement orientation are well brought out in Bernard Rosen's study in four Northeastern states of six racial and ethnic groups: French Canadians, Greeks, Southern Italians, East European Jews, Negroes, and native-born white Protestants. Four hundred twenty-seven pairs of mothers and sons, the latter generally third generation or more, were interviewed. Rosen compares these groups in achievement motivations, relevant value orientations, and aspiration levels, which, together, make up an "achievement syndrome." For each component of the syndrome, the white Protestants, Jews, and Greeks ranked higher than the French Canadians and Italians. The former groups more often imposed standards of excellence, set high goals, and expected self-reliant behavior from their children; more often upheld values that implement achievement-motivated behavior, such as individual responsibility, future planning, and active striving for goals; and had higher educational and vocational aspirations. Negroes ranked high on all these indicators except vocational aspirations.[48]

The second generation, intent upon becoming "Americanized," experiences acute conflict during the transition. The process of Americanization has usually proceeded far enough by the time of the third generation to permit that generation to feel more comfortable about the ethnic background from which it derives.

The extent to which ethnic identification persists depends upon many factors—demographic, economic, political, ideological, historical, and psychological. In New York City, the largest port of entry for ethnic groups, ethnicity remains so important that it not only influences events, "it is commonly the source of events."[49]

But although ethnic identification may persist, it changes in nature. In the first edition of their book *Beyond the Melting Pot,* published in 1963, Glazer and Moynihan argued that the national aspect of most ethnic groups rarely survives the third generation but that the groups continue because of a religious aspect, which serves as a basis of a subcommunity and subculture. The second edition, published seven years later, reports a decline in the importance of religion as a focus of ethnic identification, yet ethnic identification is reported to have renewed importance.[50]

The significance of current changes is not yet clear, but the historical trend up to now can be summarized in these terms: A situation that began with the introduction of quite different ethnic cultures has evolved into a mosaic of subcultures, all representing somewhat different versions of a larger culture. The values and norms of each subculture have distinctive implications for the socialization of its children, but in some respects the values and norms of the larger culture cut through them all.

The subcultures that provide the content of the child's socialization are brought to him by particular groups and institutions—agents of socialization, the topic to which we now turn.

5 Agencies of Socialization

Socialization occurs in many settings and in interaction with many people, organized into groupings of various kinds. Each grouping exerts particular kinds of effects on the child and each has more or less distinctive functions in preparing the child for social life. Each may therefore be called an agency of socialization.

Of course, while each agency has its own functions in socialization, functions that in certain respects may be contradictory, various agencies also reinforce each other's efforts, as was noted previously. Common cultural images of the child affect many agencies. Thus, when "getting along with others" was a dominant goal in socialization, as was true in the forties and fifties in the United States, family, school, church, voluntary associations, and even informal peer groups worked toward this end. David Riesman has given us an illuminating portrait of American society, especially middle-class society, in this period.[1] During the 1960s, socialization concerns changed in some degree; academic competence became a more important goal for many sections of both the middle and lower classes, particularly those parts of the latter made up of urban ethnic minorities. In the middle class there is also a somewhat greater emphasis on individuality and creativity as goals. These new emphases are widely diffused, so that many socialization agencies reflect the changed values and goals. Thus, family and school tend to share the increased emphasis on academic achievement, although they may often differ on implementation. Convergence and divergence of expectations coexist side by side.

Before proceeding to our discussion of particular agencies, it is important to make clear that some socialization outcomes are consciously sought by the agency of socialization, whereas others are unintended. Socialization always takes place in overlapping time frames. For example, when a parent tells a child to take his feet off the furniture, the parent is most likely concentrating on keeping the furniture clean and unscratched. The parent may or may not also be thinking at that moment about developing in the child "respect for property," "respect for authority," "self-restraint in disposing one's body," "neatness," and any number of other long-term objectives that might be considered socially desirable. But even though the parent may not have these latter objectives in mind, they may nonetheless be among the consequences of the interactions whose goal is simply to save the furniture. We are, then, alluding to an important distinction between *purpose* and *function*.[2] A purpose is a goal that a person or group wants to accomplish; it is an "end-in-view." A function is a consequence, or effect, of action and interaction. Purposes and functions may sometimes coincide; thus, knowledge of arithmetic is one of the goals, or purposes, that the elementary school endeavors to attain. It is also a function, that is, a consequence of teaching. If purposes and functions never coincided, socialization would probably be impossible. Nevertheless, it is important to bear in mind that socialization agencies have functions that are not necessarily among their purposes.

One reason functions and purposes do not entirely coincide is that although the family, school, and so on are agencies of the society, they also "have a life of their own." When we say that society—through law, custom, and public opinion—delegates certain socialization functions to specific agencies such as the family or the school, we are not describing a process that is the same as an army captain directing a subordinate to carry out an assigned task. Agencies of social-ization necessarily have more leeway in how they achieve the goals assigned to them than does the captain's aide. Agencies of socialization are accountable to the society only within rather broad limits. A school that does not include arithmetic in its curriculum will be examined by a state agency or criticized by parents, and it will be required to meet at least a minimum standard. But a great deal of what goes on in schools, in families, or in other agencies of socialization is not scrutinized, not subject to sanction by society.

It is therefore not entirely useful—but useful up to a point—to think of agencies of socialization as carrying out society's mandates. Such agencies are not like machines processing a raw material into a predetermined product. Even in a society that attempts to predetermine with great exactness the outcomes of socialization, many things go awry. As sociologist Allen Kassof observes, the efforts of the Soviet Union to mold the attitudes of its young people through closely regulated youth programs do not, for various reasons, result in uniformly starry-eyed enthusiasts. "It is too much to expect that more than a small minority should emerge from the youth program with such unblemished views of a society where the noise of busy construction is inter-rupted only by the rhythm of happy dancing and skating . . ."[3] The fact that socialization agencies develop purposes of their own and the fact that persons being socialized also develop individualities of their own should keep us from thinking too literally of society as some kind of tightly integrated "sys-tem" and from developing what sociologist Dennis Wrong has called "the oversocialized conception of man in modern sociology."[4] Although all socialization occurs through some form of interaction, and although all interaction is patterned by values and norms of some kind, interaction also evolves in directions that are not necessarily specified in advance.

The concept of "agency of socialization" needs, then, to be understood in this somewhat complex way. Any such agency generates processes, purposes, and functions of varying import. Some are most relevant to society as a whole, some to a particular subculture, some only to the agency itself. In some respects, society's mandates are quite specific and agencies are expected to be diligent in carrying them out. (For example, all families are expected to carry out society's prohibitions of incest. All elementary schools are expected to teach children to read and write. All peer groups are expected to refrain from undue violence against authority.) In other respects, society's mandates are general and even vague, leaving socialization agencies a great deal of leeway. For example, the family and the school are jointly expected to prepare children for gainful employment on reaching maturity. The school probably has more directly assigned responsibility for achieving this outcome, but the family is expected to cooperate with or at least not hamper the school in carrying out this mandate. But the mandate to the school is vague enough to be influenced by particular subcultures and by the educators in particular schools and school systems. Thus, the school may have the general obligation to help each child develop his talents to the fullest extent possible so that, among other reasons, he may qualify for "the best job" of which he is capable. But in one subculture this may mean that the school should encourage and reward capacities for independent thought, whereas in another subculture the expression of such capacities might be regarded as evidence that the school is failing in its obligation to foster respect for authority, thereby disqualifying the children for jobs as well-appreciated participants in bureaucratic organizations.

With this understanding of the complex relationship between agencies of socialization and society, let us turn to an examination of some of the most important agencies in our society.

The Family

The family is the first unit with which the child has continuous contact and the first context in which socialization patterns develop. It is a world with which he has nothing to compare and, as such, it is the most important socializing agency. True, the family is not as all-encompassing in our society as it once was, and its effects may be modified (some easily, some not so easily) by other agencies. Among many groups, children now attend nursery school or summer camps at the age of three and watch television when even younger. Schools, hospitals, government agencies, and service industries have taken over many activities that were once conducted by parents or relatives such as grandparents, uncles, and aunts. Nevertheless, despite the greater exposure of the contemporary child to outside influences, the family remains crucially important for his socialization. This may be seen from several vantage points.

The Family in the Community

The family into which he is born *places* the child in a community and in society. This means that the newborn begins his social life by acquiring the status his family has, and he will retain this status certainly throughout the first few years of his life, very probably until he reaches adulthood, and only somewhat less probably as he moves through adulthood.

To be born into a particular family, then, is to acquire a status (or set of statuses) in the community and in the society. The child's family-given status is an important determinant of the way others respond to him. The case of a boy named Johnny Rocco provides a pointed illustration:

Johnny hadn't been running the streets long when the knowledge was borne in on him that being a Rocco made him "something special"; the reputation of the notorious Roccos, known to neighbors, schools, police, and welfare agencies as "chiselers, thieves, and trouble-makers" preceded him. The cop on the beat, Johnny says, always had some cynical smart crack to make. . . . Certain children were not permitted to play with him. Wherever he went—on the streets, in the neighborhood, settlement house, at the welfare agency's penny milk station, at school, where other Roccos had been before him—he recognized himself by a gesture, an oblique remark, a wrong laugh.[5]

Although the example reveals how family notoriety may be conferred on a child who has not brought notoriety on himself, the basic principle of status-conferral holds for other kinds of statuses as well. Most importantly, the family's position in the social class structure becomes the child's position. This affects not only how he will be responded to during childhood but his adult status as well. In a large-scale study of the factors affecting occupational attainment, Peter Blau and O. D. Duncan found that "The family into which a man is born exerts a profound influence on his career, because his occupational life is conditioned by his education, and his education depends to a considerable extent on his family."[6]

The family's status in the community affects not only the way others respond to the child and the kind of formal education he is likely to receive; it also mediates for the child the culture available in the larger society. Any family participates directly in a limited number of subcultures and networks (one based on social class position, one based on ethnic-group membership, possibly others based on kinship, occupations, or interests). These are the versions of the larger society that are made most directly available to the child through example, teaching, and taken-for-granted daily activity. At the same time, any family is likely to be aware of at least portions of other subcultures that may serve as subjects of emulation or derogatory comment. In these ways, the family into which the child is born presents him with selective versions of the larger society, with the result that the child may early become impressed with the importance of religious devotion, or baseball, or school achievement, or sexual intercourse as a primary focus of attention, depending upon the emphasis of the subculture(s) in which his family participates. In sum, the family is not simply a passive transmitter of a subculture to its children but plays an active part in screening in and screening out elements of available subcultures. This is accomplished (1) by means of activities—for example, going to church, inviting guests, visiting friends, going to football games—and (2) through comment and comparison—evaluating such activities and the people who do or do not participate in them and evaluating the groups and subcultures of which these activities are a part.[7]

The family's position in the community affects the age-grading of children. This is to say that what is expected of a child at given ages depends to some extent on his family's social position. Families thus differ in the rate at which they *pace* their children toward maturity. Generally, childhood is of longer duration in middle-class than in lower-class families. In the latter children take on serious responsibilities at an earlier age. For example, in a study of very poor black families living in a public housing project, David Schulz found that first-born daughters are given responsibility for caring for their younger siblings when they themselves are very young and, by the age of nine, may even be doing much of the grocery shopping and cooking in their households.[8] Although later-born girls are less likely to have as heavy responsibilities caring for younger siblings, they are likely, as is their eldest sister, to begin having children of their own when in their early or middle teens. Child-care responsibilities thus begin at a much earlier age than is the case in the middle class, whether Negro or white. In a sociological sense, it can be said that childhood ends at an earlier age.

In Schulz's findings we see an illustration of the distinction between intended and unintended outcomes of socialization. The mothers intend that their first-born girls take care of younger siblings and also become competent in shopping and cooking. The mothers do not, however, wish to see their daughters begin giving birth to children of their own in their teens and, indeed, endeavor, however ineffectively, to prevent this from occurring. But since the mothers themselves began having children when they were adolescent, they provide models with which their daughters identify and which, therefore, weaken the impact of their strictures. Further, the subculture does not apply strong negative sanctions against early motherhood, in or out of wedlock. Most importantly, the pervasive discrimination practiced by whites against Negroes, and especially against those who are poor, functions in various ways to prevent many young and poor black girls from developing effective goals for adulthood that would enable them to delay motherhood. Becoming a mother provides some feeling of self-esteem in a subculture with many deprivations and many norms shaped by discrimination.[9]

In sum, then, a child is born into a family, and his family gives him his location in society. From the moment of his birth, before he has had the opportunity to take any actions on his own, the child is located in society—as middle class or working class, child of a teacher or truck driver, Christian or Jew, member of a dominant or a subordinate ethnic group, member of a family respected or scorned by neighbors. His family's—and therefore his—location in these social groupings affects the experiences he will have as he matures. It will determine, to a significant degree, not only what form his socialization opportunities will take, but also at what ages, in what order, and with whom. It will also play an important part, as Blau and Duncan note, in determining his later location in society when he has become an adult.

The Family As an Interaction Structure

Although one of the family's functions is to place the child in the society and thereby directly or indirectly affect his experiences outside the home, this is not its only importance in socialization. The family has an organization of its own which has its own direct effects on the child.[10]

From this perspective, perhaps the most important function of the family in socialization is that it introduces the child to intimate and personal relationships. Since his first social relationships are family relationships, it is in this group that he acquires his first experiences of being treated as a person in his own right. He receives care for his dependency and attention for his sociability. Because the newborn child is both without experience and very needing of care and attention, his initial outlook is assumed to be, loosely, egocentric. The kind of care and attention he receives during his first and second years of life affects his resolution of the issues of trust versus distrust and autonomy versus shame and doubt —and therefore his capacity for establishing later ties with people outside his family.

At the outset the newborn is unaware that he is a separate and distinct person. As time goes on, he becomes aware, first, that he and his mother (or other care-taking persons) are separate and, then, that there are other members of the household—father and, possibly, siblings. He learns that they each have wishes, interests, and ways of their own and that it is to his advantage to adapt to them. Their appreciation of him and his needs and wishes is not invariable— indeed it varies according to his responsiveness to them. Living in a household shared with others, the child learns that he must share the resources of the household—the space, the furnishings and other objects, the time and attention of parents and siblings. He learns the ways in which his cooperation is sought and welcomed and the ways in which he may compete for what he wants when it conflicts with what other family members want. In interacting with him, parents may be more or less expressive of their feelings, more or less authoritative, more or less protective. The mother, in dressing a young child, may demand or plead for his cooperation; the father, in disciplining the child, may be angry or businesslike. Siblings may be more or less jealous, more or less interested in accepting him as a playmate and companion.

Through these various kinds of interaction with family members—such as being cared for, being disciplined, being accepted as a companion and playmate—the child develops his initial capacities for establishing relationships with others. These capacities will find both later expression and further development in relationships with nonfamily playmates, co-workers, authority figures, friends, and, ultimately, his spouse and his own children.[11]

The family into which he is born is the child's first reference group, the first group whose values, norms, and practices he refers to in evaluating his own behavior. What this implies, as Talcott Parsons and Robert F. Bales have argued, is that the child identifies with the family as a group, so that its ways become part of his own self. These authors have thus amplified the concept of identification beyond the original meaning Freud gave it when he spoke of the child as identifying with the parent of the same sex.[12] This means, for example, that not only do the particular members of the family constitute models for the child's own behavior but *the pattern of interaction among the members* itself becomes a model. The child's socialization is affected not merely by having a hard-working or an alcoholic father, a loving or indifferent mother, a domineering or distant older sibling. It is affected also by whether the interaction in the family is characteristically relaxed and good-natured or tense and guarded, whether it emphasizes or minimizes the distance between parents and children or between males and females, whether it is typically cooperative or competitive.

One way of describing differences in family interaction patterns has been proposed by Herbert Gans, who suggests that there are three main types of family in North America. The *adult-centered* family is "run by adults for adults, . . . the role of the children is to behave as much as possible like miniature adults." In this type of family, children and their wishes are clearly subordinate to parents and theirs. Children are expected to conduct themselves in ways pleasing to adults and not make themselves intrusive. Parents in these families are not very self-conscious or purposive in their child rearing. They

are not concerned with *developing* their children, that is, with raising them in accordance with a predetermined goal or target which they are expected to achieve. [They] have no clear image of the future social status, occupational level, or life-style that they want their children to reach. And even when they do, they do not know how to build it into the child-rearing process.[13]

In the *child-centered* family, parents are more attentive to the child. In this type of family, unlike the adult-centered, children are planned, and the parents' educational aspirations influence how many children they will have. In the child-centered type, family companionship is prominent; parents spend time playing with their children and give up some adult pleasures for them. They want their children to have a happier childhood than they had. The fathers assume that their children will be occupationally successful, at least matching and hopefully surpassing the parental occupational achievement. In contrast, in the adult-centered family there is more concern about downward social mobility, with the parents seeking reassurance that the child's conduct is sufficiently satisfactory to prevent him from becoming a "bum."

The third type of family Gans calls *adult-directed.* Parents are generally college-educated and know what they want for their children much more clearly than do parents in the child-centered type. Emphasis is placed on individual growth. Children are taught to strive for self-development in accordance with their own individuality.

Gans finds that each of these three types of family is most characteristic of a particular social class. The adult-directed pattern is more common in the upper-middle class, the child-centered in the lower-middle class, and the adult-centered in the working class. Weller concluded that the adult-centered type, which Gans found among working-class Italian-Americans in Boston, also typified the Anglo-Saxon mountain people in Appalachia.[14]

Although family interaction styles unquestionably tend to vary with social class, it also needs to be said that insufficient attention has been paid to variations *within* a social class or other social category. When such variation is the focus of research attention, the results suggest how family interaction patterns have effects on socialization that do not derive from social class. Norman Bell, for example, studied a group of working-class families half of which had an emotionally disturbed child. He found that in the families with a disturbed child, relatives tended to be drawn into family conflicts in ways that exacerbated the conflicts, evidently with some impact on the child, whereas the families without a disturbed child were able to limit involvement of extended kin.[15]

One other aspect of family structure needs to be considered: the significance of persons in specific family statuses. The importance of the mother has been discussed in an earlier chapter. At this point we need only reiterate that the mother is ordinarily the first socializing agent. As such, she is the first representative of society to the child and, through the care she provides, initiates the development of the sentiments and symbols that give the child his human nature and enable him to become a responsive participant in society.

The father's contribution to the child's socialization has received much less systematic attention. As Leonard Benson observes, "Mother is the primary parent. She is first by popular acclaim, in actual household practice, and in the minds of students of family life . . . material on mother is much more extensive than that on fathers."[16] Nevertheless, certain ideas and findings about the father's importance have emerged.

One way in which the father is important, according to Talcott Parsons' analysis, is that his presence and participation in the family help the child to relinquish his dependency on the mother. At first the father tends to be regarded as "an intruder" into the close initial mother-child relationship. He is the main source of pressure for the child to modify his early love attachment to the mother, although she also works toward such modification. After a while the child identifies with the father; one result of this is that the child himself works toward loosening his attachment to his mother. Further, since the father usually works and spends less time at home than the mother, he comes to be seen as a representative of the outside world and of "the higher demands" that the child is progressively required to meet. In this way the father is significant in turning the child's attention to the adult world outside the family and in expanding his horizon.[17]

Although the father's authority in the family is less absolute than it once was, Benson argues that the father still plays a decisive part in communicating to the child a sense of social order. In Benson's words:

Father's influence on the social climate within which his children's many experiences occur is perhaps most important. It establishes the conditions for his basic value, or moral, function: to develop a generalized commitment to social order. His existence personifies for his children the inevitability of rules. . . . Of course the rules are implicit in the ordered behavior of almost everyone who enters the life of the growing child, but father commonly comes to "stand for" the absolute necessity of social order more than any other person. Even the social pattern that mother establishes is typically legitimized by the larger, more insistent parent lurking in the background.[18]

Not least important, the father provides a basic model of masculinity. For his sons, this model becomes a basis for developing their own male identity. For his daughters, the model provides a basis for developing images of male companions and perhaps a desirable husband. For children of both sexes, these images are influenced not only by the father's actual conduct but by the mother's evaluations of him as well. Further, there is evidence that the father's status in the outside world affects the way his children perceive him. One study of boys in the age bracket of nine to eleven found that middle-class boys tend to perceive their fathers as ambitious, competent, and successful; as interested in their performance in school and in other settings; and as responsive to requests for attention. Lower-class boys tended to see their fathers quite differently—as nervous, shy, and worried.[19]

In a variety of ways, then, the father is one of the child's most important links to the world that lies beyond the family.

Finally, in discussing the effects of family statuses on socialization, it should be pointed out that there is also some evidence that the size and composition of the sibling group affects socialization. James Bossard and Eleanor Boll compared one hundred families each with two children with one hundred families each of which had six or more children. They found that there tended to be more "regimentation" and assigning of jobs in the large families than in the small and that in the small families "the children were often spared from all household chores in the interests of concentrating on their education, outside activities, and social life."[20] They also reported that siblings in the small families were more dependent upon their parents for security, whereas the children in the large families were more likely to find security "in the numbers of siblings who formed a cohesive group for defense, playing, confiding, teaching, even plotting against parents."

Bossard and Boll point to a greater probability that the small family will have children all of one sex, and they cite census figures which report that 29 percent of American families have only girls, 30 percent only boys, and 41 percent, the minority, have children of both sexes.[21] Their emphasis on the fact that many children do not have the experience of growing up in a house with siblings of the opposite sex gains significance from the work of sociologist Orville Brim.

Brim examined data collected by psychologist Helen Koch in a large study of personality traits of children in two-child families. Making use of George Herbert Mead's theory of social interaction, Brim reasoned that "taking the role of the other" should result in a greater frequency of typical cross-sex personality traits in children who have a sibling of the opposite sex than in children whose only sibling is of the same sex. When he examined Koch's data from this perspective, he found that his prediction was substantially correct. Thus, a girl with a brother was more likely to have "high masculinity traits" (such as ambition or competitiveness) than a girl whose sibling is another girl. Similarly, the boy whose sibling is a sister is somewhat more likely to show "high femininity traits" (such as affectionateness or obedience) than the boy whose sibling is a brother. These results suggest that the learning of sex roles is affected by the composition of the sibling group within the family. Brim cautions that the particular effects he found are limited to two-child families and that sibships of different composition would very likely result in different patterns. Nevertheless, Brim argues, sibling relations are important for sex-role learning. Although the parents are the major sources of sex-role learning, *variations* in this learning must be due in part to sibling differences (along with such other factors as the sex of neighborhood playmates), since most children have a mother and father to learn from.[22]

The School

The importance of the school as an agency of socialization has already been suggested in several illustrations. Now we wish to treat this agency more systematically. For the sake of convenience, we shall divide our discussion into three sub-topics: the school and society, the classroom, and the teacher. Although this division is somewhat artificial because each of these subtopics is fully understandable only in relation to the others, the distinctions will nevertheless be helpful in organizing our discussion.

School and Society

When he begins to go to school, the child ordinarily comes, for the first time, under the supervision of people who are not his kin. He thus moves from a milieu dominated by personal ties to one that is more impersonal (although the degree of impersonality is theoretically less at the kindergarten level than it becomes later). By involving the child with teachers and classmates, the school plays an important part in lessening the child's emotional dependence on his family. Furthermore, the school is likely to be the first agency (in a literate society)—except perhaps for the church —which stimulates the child to develop loyalties and sentiments that go beyond the family, that link the child to a wider social order. The school is society's principal agency— at least its principal formally designated agency—for loosening the child's ties to his parents and initiating him into social institutions that cut across kin and neighborhood groupings.

The school as an agency of socialization needs to be recognized, then, first as an organizer of social relationships and stimulator of sentiments. Some of the social relationships will be discussed in the following section on the classroom. As an example of its role in organizing sentiments we may observe how the school stimulates loyalty to the existing political and social order. One study of 12,000 children from second through eighth grades concludes that

The school apparently plays the largest part in teaching attitudes, conceptions, and beliefs about the operation of the political system. While it may be argued that the family contributes much to the socialization that goes into basic loyalty to the country, the school gives content, information, and concepts which expand and elaborate these early feelings of attachment.[23]

This study also suggests that the school places greater emphasis on compliance with law, authority, and school regulations than on the rights and obligations of a citizen to participate in government. Neither does it promote the child's understanding of the efficacy of group action or other legitimate ways of influencing government.

Orienting the child to and fostering his respect for the established social and political order is one of the ways in which the school functions as a conservative socializing agency. It seeks to pass on to the child the knowledge, sentiments, skills, and values that have been built up over time and presumably thereby provide him with the resources he will need in his adult roles. At the same time, there is growing recognition that the pace of social change in contemporary industrialized societies is so rapid that transmitting a particular heritage of the past is not sufficient for socialization. A British professor states flatly that "In most countries of the world nearly all the education consciously given is already out of date. It is sometimes out of date at the time when education is taking place. It is more usually out of date in terms of the children's prospects."[24] A more complex picture is provided by an American sociologist who argues with reference to the United States that

> as a society we have decreed that the responsibility of our schools shall not end with the maintenance of the status quo nor even with the socialization of individuals who are able to adapt easily to a changing social and physical environment, but instead shall extend to the maximum encouragement of the creative abilities of new members of the society. Thus, paradoxically, educational institutions have assumed a major role as agents of innovation and change along with their conservative role in assuring the cultural continuity of the society.[25]

He further argues that many of the issues in American education can be understood as debates over the relative weight that should be given to the school's conservative as opposed to its innovative function. Many observers have pointed out that socializing children for a society in such rapid change is a new task, one not encountered by any society before, and it is not surprising that no one is entirely sure how to do it. The problem is exacerbated by the fact that the school seems to change more slowly than other aspects of the society.[26] There are undoubtedly many reasons for this, among them being school responsiveness to conservative community pressure. Such pressure in part can be understood in terms of socialization, for socialization has the general effect of giving people a more definite picture of society as they *have* experienced it than as they *will* experience it in the future. Community pressures on the school system to socialize children for society as it has been known are therefore likely to be generally stronger than pressures to socialize for a society whose form is as yet unknown.

Although the British professor quoted above may be correct that almost all education is out of date by the time it is to be used, many observers note that the schools nevertheless seem to prepare some children better than others, whether preparation be defined in minimal terms as learning to "read, write, and reckon" or in more sophisticated terms such as learning how to cope with unforeseen problems. The reasons for this are multiple and complex, and a full exploration would take us far beyond the scope of this book. But the basic situation can be summed up as follows: *The effectiveness of the school as a socializing agency depends to a major degree upon the kind of family its children come from.* Generally, the school tends to be less effective in educating children from families that are poor and of low status. Such children are often, though by no means invariably, from minority groups. Although there is wide agreement that schools are not as successful in socializing children from poor and low-status families as they are with those of higher income and status, there is wide disagreement concerning the causes of the discrepancy. Some observers attribute it to differences in what the schools give the children, whereas others attribute it to what the children bring to the school in the way of home-based socialization. There is evidence to support both viewpoints.

Considerable evidence has accumulated by now to indicate that the American school tends to reinforce the child's family-given status. This is brought about in a number of direct and indirect ways. Schools in neighborhoods where poor families predominate tend to receive smaller allocations of educational resources than those in higher income and status neighborhoods.[27] Schools that serve children of various status levels and that also have more than one classroom or section for each grade level tend to group the children in sections according to the status of their families, even though ability or achievement is the ostensible basis for grouping. In Britain, too, a study reports that

although teachers genuinely intended to stream children according to their measured ability, they nonetheless allowed these judgments to be influenced by the type of home the children came from. . . . Even where children *of the same level of ability* are considered, those from middle-class homes tended to be allocated to the upper streams and those from the manual working-class to the lower streams. Furthermore, children who were dirty or badly clothed or who came from large families also tended to be placed in lower streams, regardless of ability.[28]

Thus, children of lower social status tend to be perceived by school personnel as having less ability to benefit from education than children of higher status.

Teachers in schools where pupils are predominantly lower status are more likely to be lower in morale and to seek transfer to "more desirable" schools than teachers in schools where pupils are predominantly middle class.[29] Teacher dissatisfaction in these schools with lower-status pupils appears to be related to the fact that academic performance of pupils is lower in these schools. So we see what appears to be a circular and self-continuing process: Low-status children tend not to learn as much as those of higher status, thereby arous-

ing discontent in their teachers, which impairs teacher performance and which further depresses pupil achievement.[30]
Various studies thus strongly suggest that the school does
not put forth its best efforts in educating pupils from poor
and low-status families.

Other studies, not necessarily inconsistent with the above,
suggest that such pupils tend to fare poorly in school partly
because they begin school poorly prepared by their early
socialization in the family. These children are seen as deprived of the kinds of experiences that would enable them to
take advantage of what the school has to offer. Many studies
point to the deprivation that derives from inadequate experience in using language, perhaps because the home is generally lacking in stimulation[31] or perhaps because the mother's
language in interacting with her child provides him with
diminished opportunity for thinking and making choices.[32]

An interesting variant of this point of view is proposed by
Fred L. Strodtbeck. He agrees that the financially poor home
provides a language-deprived environment for the child, as
compared to the middle-class home, but he argues that the
main reason is that the very poor family, especially one without a father, provides a much simpler role organization. The
middle-class home provides a "hidden curriculum" that
teaches the child to use language with finesse in order to
get what he wants:

> . . . the presence of both a father and a mother who are
> relatively equal in power provides a child with a motivation to
> attend closely to the state of normative integration. . . . The
> existence of two persons of power with small value differences,
> yet parallel commitment to a core of common values, creates a
> situation in which careful use of language and recognition of
> subtle differences is required to attain personal goals.[33]

In sum, the school is organized in a way that assumes a
certain kind of preschool socialization in the family. Children
from poor and low-status families often seem not to have
this preparation, but the school has only recently begun to

change its organization (allocation of funds and personnel, methods of teaching, curriculum, and so on) in an effort to improve its performance in educating them. Also, the schools often exacerbate the problem by assuming that poor and low-status children are difficult to educate, even when this is not the case.

While the school generally functions to sustain children in the statuses to which they are born, it also functions to encourage upward mobility. Children who do well in school, whatever their family backgrounds, are likely to win awards and to be encouraged to go on to higher education. One study estimates that 5 percent of American university students during the 1950s came from lower-working-class families and 25 percent from upper-working-class families.[34] There is some evidence that communities vary in the extent to which they offer equality of educational opportunity, regardless of a child's family background.[35]

The Classroom and Socialization

For the young child the school classroom constitutes a social situation without parallel. Ordinarily a student spends about 1,000 hours per year in a classroom, and he will spend approximately 7,000 hours in school between kindergarten and the end of the sixth grade. Except for sleeping, no other activity or enclosure will claim as much of his time.[36]

The structure of the classroom has both short-run and long-run implications for the child. Since most of what a child does in a classroom is done in the presence of others, he has to learn to cope with a more or less formalized multiperson situation. He has to learn to wait his turn, and this means not only waiting to satisfy his wishes to speak or perform but often abandoning those wishes if the activity moves on to something else. Also, the child must learn to ignore those around him and not be distracted by them. As one observer of classroom functioning notes:

. . . if students are to face the demands of classroom life with
equanimity they must learn to be patient. This means that they
must be able to disengage, at least temporarily, their feelings
from their actions. It also means . . . that they must be able to
re-engage feelings and actions when conditions are appropriate.
In other words, students must wait patiently for their turn to
come, but when it does they must still be capable of zestful
participation. They must accept the fact of not being called on
during a group discussion, but they must continue to volunteer.
. . . In most classrooms, powerful social sanctions are in operation to force the student to maintain an attitude of patience. If
he impulsively steps out of line, his classmates are likely to
complain about his being selfish or "pushy." If he shifts over
into a state of overt withdrawal, his teacher is apt to call him
back to active participation.[37]

This is a good illustration of how the child is induced to sustain responsive participation in society, which we discussed
briefly in Chapter 3.

The time schedule that governs classroom activities has
another effect on the child: The beginning and ending of
activities does not necessarily correspond to the child's interest in them. They may begin before he is interested and may
end before he has lost interest—sometimes "when it's just
getting interesting."

These various aspects of adapting to the crowded classroom—learning to delay or suppress desires, to tolerate
interruptions, and to turn aside from distractions—are part
of what is referred to as the classroom's "hidden curriculum." This term is gaining favor as a way of calling attention
to the informal and unofficial matters that are taught, matters
generally unnoticed by those who have responsibility for
teaching the official curriculum. While the pupil is learning
skills (such as reading and handwriting) and subjects (such
as arithmetic and geography), he is also interacting with his
fellow pupils and teacher in ways that strengthen his membership in society.

Since pupils differ in the rate and quality of their learning
and in the various kinds of social facility that are encouraged
in the classroom (for example, promptness, cooperativeness,

and cheerfulness), their progress toward desired goals is evaluated. Although the teacher is the main source of evaluation, the child also evaluates himself—he knows when he can't spell a word or solve a problem. Also, the class as a whole may be asked to evaluate a student's work, "as when the teacher asks, 'Who can correct Billy?' or 'How many believe that Shirley read that poem with a lot of expression?' "[38] The classroom environment is one in which a child is being evaluated in a variety of ways—by teacher comments, self-judgments, classmate judgments, report cards, marks and comments (and perhaps gold stars, red stars, or blue stars) on exercises and papers, classroom displays of the "best" papers, requests that he stay after school or bring his parents in for a conference. Sometimes there is organized competition (as in spelling bees, which may pit boys against girls, thus emphasizing sex identity along with competitiveness and learning of the official curricular material), which adds to the evaluational process.

This ongoing and multifaceted process of evaluation contributes to socialization in two main ways. The first is that *the evaluations become processed into the child's developing self.* He learns certain of society's values and norms, and in this way his self is transformed: He learns to be neat, prompt, able to follow instructions, and so forth—or he learns that he is not very good at being neat or prompt or at following instructions. He learns to think of himself as being good in math or not so good in math, good or not so good in reading, and so on. These evaluations of his achievements in skills, subject matters, and social performances thus gradually accrue to his emerging self. The child thus comes to know himself as a particular kind of social being, one who may aspire to certain kinds of future opportunities but not to others.

While his self is thus evolving, the child is also acquiring a certain kind of reputation among teachers and a "cumulative record" which is semipublic.[39] The quality of this record (and reputation) serves as a ticket of admission (or refusal) for later opportunities, and this is the second main way in which evaluation affects socialization. At any given point during the formation of his reputation and record, their quality at that point affects the child's progression to the next step—for example, whether he will be put into a fast, slow, or average section, whether he is doing well enough in classwork to be allowed participation in school team sports, whether he has done well enough in lower grades to be admitted to college-preparatory curricula in high school, whether he has done well enough in high school to be admitted to a college (and, if so, to what kind of college, with how much encouragement in the way of scholarships, and the like). In short, the school classroom functions as a system of selection for sequences of interlocking opportunities leading to particular kinds of adult roles.[40]

The Teacher's Functions

Many readers of this book will perhaps recall a particular elementary school teacher as especially influential or helpful; other readers will have no such recollections, all their teachers being dimly fused in one anonymous blur. How influential are teachers? Is there any evidence—apart from subjective recall—that teachers can be significant in the socialization of children? Some recent research suggests that they can be.

One study of particular interest examines and tests a basic sociological axiom formulated by W. I. Thomas: "If men define situations as real, they are real in their consequences." In a somewhat elaborated formulation, the process has been called "the self-fulfilling prophecy."[41] This means that one's beliefs lead one to act in such a way that the beliefs cannot help but be reaffirmed. The study by Robert Rosenthal and Lenore Jacobson explores "how one person's expectations for another person's behavior can quite unwittingly become a more accurate prediction simply for its having been made," and it asks specifically "whether a teacher's expectation for her pupils' intellectual competence can come to serve as an educational self-fulfilling prophecy."[42] To test the validity of this idea, the investigators conducted an experiment in a school whose pupils were mostly of lower-class background. First, they administered to all the pupils an intelligence test, which they disguised with the highfalutin name "Harvard Test of Inflected Acquisition." They told the teachers that this test could predict academic "blooming" or "spurting," and they asked the teachers not to discuss the test with pupils or parents. Then, in a completely random way entirely unconnected with the test results, the names of about 20 percent of the students were selected and, at the beginning of the following school year, given to their teachers with the explanation that they might like to know which of their pupils were "about to bloom." Since the names of these pupils were drawn from a hat, in effect, "the difference between the children earmarked for intellectual growth and the undesignated control children was in the mind of the teacher."[43] Retesting showed that at the end of the school year the children with the "special" designation gained an average of more than twelve IQ points, whereas the others averaged a gain of about eight points. The differences were much greater than this at the first and second grade levels than at higher grades. Further, later retesting when the children had moved on to new teachers indicated that there was some persistence in the differential gain. Significantly, then, children who were expected by their teachers to "bloom" did so, much more than those for whom teachers did not have this expectation; and the younger the children, the greater was the effect of the teacher's expectation.

Exactly what went on between teacher and pupils to bring about these results is not clear, but the investigators suggest three possible explanations of the differences between age groups: (1) Since younger children are less fixed and more capable of change, they are more subject to the effects of "critical periods"; (2) younger children are less well known and have less firmly established reputations in a school, so that their teachers are more inclined to take somebody's word about a child's promise for blooming than are third- to fifth-grade teachers, who have confidence in reputations already established; (3) the effects of the teachers' expectancies may be greater on the younger children than the older ones, not because they really are more malleable, but because teachers *believe* that they are.

Although the precise reason for differential change at different age levels remains uncertain, the study not only provides evidence that teacher expectations can have significant effects on socialization but also supports other work that indicates that a child's intelligence is not fixed at birth but is a complex product of his innate capacities and his experience."

If teachers' expectations can be so influential as strongly to influence a child's very intelligence, and if the classroom is one of the important places in which the child competes and is prepared for his adult statuses and roles, it is pertinent to ask whether children in one classroom have as good a chance as children in another to come under the influence of teachers who will have favorable expectations. Or, conversely, is there some social process at work that tends to make it more likely that certain kinds of children will come under the influence of teachers with less favorable expectations and that they will accordingly experience less "bloom-promoting" teacher-pupil interaction? We provided a partial answer to this question when we cited a study showing that teachers in schools with predominantly lower-class pupils are more likely to want transfers out. From this and other related studies we could infer that the children of these teachers tend to be evaluated more negatively than middle-class children. But can we go beyond inference and actually see teachers communicating different kinds of expectations to children, based on the children's status?

A recent study by anthropologist Eleanor Leacock examines this question.[45] She observed second- and fifth-grade classrooms and interviewed the teachers and pupils in four city schools, each located in a different kind of neighborhood. The predominant pupil background of the four schools was, respectively, lower-income Negro, lower-income white, middle-income Negro, middle-income white. Although she found certain similarities in the four schools—traceable to such factors as similar teacher training, similar educational philosophy, and the fact that the schools were all part of the same school system and therefore subject to similar administrative practices—certain differences were also significant.

The differences Leacock found among the teachers do *not* fall into any simple pattern; she did not find that all the "bad" aspects of teaching were in the lowest-status classrooms and the "good" aspects in the higher-status ones. For example, the second-grade teachers were somewhat more positive than fifth-grade teachers in evaluating pupil participation, and this was as true in the low-income Negro school as in any of the others. Teacher pleasantness or unpleasantness to pupils was unrelated to the status of the pupils in this study, as also was teacher competence. But one difference that did emerge was that teachers seemed to expect less of their pupils if they were from the low-income group. In the middle-income schools, the teachers were likely to work more actively with a child having difficulty with a problem, whereas those in the low-income schools would more quickly give up and turn to another child, making little effort to see that the first child understood. At the fifth-grade level the teacher in the low-income Negro school was observed to have difficulty explaining arithmetic, but made the pupils seem responsible for failure to understand. One general conclusion reached by the study goes counter to some currently fashionable interpretations of school life:

What we observed in the [low-income Negro] classroom was not the attempt to "impose middle-class goals" on the children but rather a tacit assumption that these goals were not open to at least the vast majority of them. *The "middle-class values" being imposed on the low-income Negro children defined them as inadequate and their proper role as one of deference.* Despite the fact that some teachers in the low-income schools stated their felt responsibility to set "middle-class standards" for the children, their lowered expectations were expressed by a low emphasis on goal-setting statements altogether. In a three-hour period, clear-cut overt goal-setting statements numbered 12 and 13 for the low-income Negro school, 15 and 18 for the low-income white school, and 43 and 46 for the middle-income white school.[46]

Thus, the evidence of this and other studies converges to suggest that pupils from low-income and low-status families are more likely to be met by lower levels of expectation for accomplishment from their teachers. The likely result of these lower levels of expectation is a reduction in levels of aspiration, levels of accomplishment, and probably even levels of intelligence.

The Peer Group

While the family and the school are socializing agencies organized primarily by adults, the child also comes to be socialized into a world in which adults are peripheral. This world is generally designated by the term *peer group*. The term is a bit misleading, since it does not designate a single group in which a child participates but rather all those groups made up of children in which any particular child participates. Any given child is likely to belong to more than one peer group, although there may be overlapping membership. Thus, one peer group may consist of the children on his block or in his apartment building. Another may include his playmates at school. A third may be the children in the same Boy Scout troop or those who go to the same summer camp or music school. Yet another may be made up of his cousins whom he may see as a group at periodic intervals. It would therefore be more accurate to speak of the child's "peer world," since his actual peer groups might differ in significant ways and the child might have different roles within them. For example, adult values might be more prominent in a Boy Scout or Girl Scout troop than in the neighborhood backyard or back alley peer group. We shall use the conventional term, however, and the reader will be able to judge from the context when we are referring to a particular type of peer group and when we are more generally discussing the peer world.

The peer group as a socializing agency has certain distinctive characteristics: (1) By definition, it is made up of members who have about the same age status; (2) within the peer group the members have varying degrees of prestige and power; (3) the peer group is centered about its own concerns. Whereas adult authority figures instruct the child in traditional norms and values with an awareness that the child must learn to function in adult society, the peer group has no such responsibility. (4) Thus, any long-run socializing implications are largely unintentional. The child participating in his peer group does not do so with the aim of preparing himself for adult society, though his peer group experiences do have such import.

The child's peer group participation may be said to begin in a very rudimentary way in the sandbox at about the age of two. As the child develops, he participates in a succession of peer groups. With increasing age, peer groups gain in organization, and usually in size, while the activities and interests on which they focus change with maturation and social development.

The Peer Culture

While children are absorbing the adult culture at home and in the school, they also sustain a subculture of their own, a subculture that is age-limited. The richness of this subculture is suggested by studies conducted in Britain by Iona and

Peter Opie. One of these reports on some 2,500 games played by children ages six to twelve. While many of these are simply slight regional variants of basic games (none of which requires even such minimal equipment as a ball), children nonetheless sustain a great variety of games that can be roughly classified into eleven different types: chasing, catching, seeking, hunting, racing, duelling, exerting, daring, acting, guessing, and pretending. Excluded from the study were party games, scout games, team games, and any sport that required supervision.

This study, carried out over a ten-year period in many parts of Britain, discloses that certain kinds of rules appear repeatedly. There are, for example, rules for starting a game. Two or three children on a street or playground initiate the idea and then, to round up enough to play, they issue a traditional "summons" to others around. In one region, for example, children call out, "All in, all in, a bottle of gin; all out, all out, a bottle of stout."[47] While there is considerable local variation in the particular wording of the call, the practice of some such traditional way of starting a game is widespread.

Similarly, there are rules for avoidance of a disliked role. The investigators observed that

the chief impediment to a swift start is the fact that in most games one player has to take a part that is different from the rest; and all children have, or affect to have, an insurmountable objection to being the first one to take this part. Tradition, if not inclination, demands that they do whatever they can to avoid being the chaser, or the seeker, or the one who . . . is "it."[48]

To avoid being first, children shout out some particular phrase or engage in some particular gesture. By general agreement, the last one to do so is first to be "it." And just as there are rules for choosing the first child who will be in a role that pits him against the others, so there are rules for changing roles. Thus, in chasing games, a touch results in a change of role.

It appears that games of this kind were once played by grown-ups and children together and that they did not become distinctively children's games until about the start of the eighteenth century.[47] Today they are virtually restricted to children and taught by children. The rules are sustained by children, as is the interest in them. The Opies note that games go through periods of rise and decline in popularity and comment that

> it is no coincidence that the games whose decline is most pronounced are those which are best known to adults, and therefore the most often promoted by them; while the games and amusements that flourish are those that adults find most difficulty in encouraging (e.g., knife-throwing games and chases in the dark) . . .[50]

In an earlier study the same investigators documented a vast amount of lore and language known mostly to children and evidently circulated largely by them. This takes such various forms as "petty verbal stratagems," riddles, parodies, "codes of oral legislation" (such as "finders keepers, losers weepers"), jeers and torments, secret languages, and many others.[51] The study turned up many parallels in the United States and some on the European continent, suggesting that at least certain aspects of the peer culture transcend ethnic and national boundaries.

On street and playground, children sustain a subculture. It consists of rules, traditions, language, interests and activities, and ways of making and breaking peer relationships that are somewhat apart from, and sometimes in opposition to, the subcultures the children are simultaneously absorbing from adult models and institutions.

Although our attention will focus now on the distinctive functions of the peer group considered as a world separate from that of adults, it should be remembered that some peer groups are organized around adult values and draw upon adult models. In our discussion of middle-class subculture we mentioned that children participate in many groups sponsored and controlled by adults. Working-class children also participate in such groups, often based in such institutions as churches, settlement houses, scout troops, and Little League baseball teams. Parental encouragement is often considerable. It should also be noted that parents sometimes intervene in child-organized peer groups, for example, by prohibiting their child to play with another child or participate in a group that they consider undesirable, while encouraging him to play with others they consider more suitable. Such parental intervention is often based on social class and ethnic evaluations, with the result that the child is led unwittingly to take on parental sentiments and attitudes toward other social classes and ethnic groups.

Functions of the Peer Group

Philippe Ariès has stated that "The development of mass education is undoubtedly the most important social change that has ever taken place."[52] The reason he gives such emphasis to this development is that it had the effect of setting children apart from adults, of making them a special group in society. True as this is, and significant as it is, this judgment overlooks the fact that the school is organized by adults and is specifically governed by the purpose of preparing children for adult life. So while the children are defined as a group apart, the school does not really keep them apart from adults and the adult world. The only social setting in which children are in fact separated from adults in any meaningful sense is in the peer group, governed as it is by the rules, rituals, interests, and logics of children. From this point of view, then, it would seem that one of the functions of the peer group is to keep children from being completely immersed in the process of socialization. But this conclusion must be qualified. Although it is probably true that the peer group retards socialization in the sense of keeping the child from being totally concerned by the rules, values, and norms of the adult world, there are other ways in which it contributes to socialization.

First, the peer group gives the child experience in egalitarian types of relationships. In this group he engages in a process of give-and-take not ordinarily possible in his relationships with adults. In the family and in school the child is necessarily a subordinate to parents and teachers (however benign his subordination may be). In the peer group he gains his first substantial experience of equality. The child entering a peer group is interested in the companionship, attention, and good will of the group (particularly of the members of the group who are significant for him), and the group is in a position to satisfy this interest. For behaving in the appropriate or valued manner, the group rewards its members by bestowing attention, approval, or leadership or by giving permission to participate or to employ certain symbols. For behaving otherwise, the peer group punishes by disdain, ostracism, or other expressions of disapproval. As with other socializing agencies, the child comes to view himself as an object from the point of view of the group and in some measure to internalize its standards. While he is a member, these standards are reinforced by the feelings of solidarity and support that he obtains from others.

The way in which games contribute to this process has been nicely described:

> . . . the child disclose[s] his unsureness of his place in the world by welcoming games with set procedures, in which his relationships with his fellows are clearly established. In games, a child can exert himself without having to explain himself, he can be a good player without having to think whether he is a popular person, he can find himself being a useful partner to someone of whom he is ordinarily afraid. He can be confident, too, in particular games, that it is his place to issue commands, to inflict pain, to steal people's possessions, to pretend to be dead, to hurl a ball actually at someone, to pounce on someone, or to kiss someone he has caught. In ordinary life either he never knows these experiences or, by attempting them, he makes himself an outcast.[53]

A second function of the peer group stems from the fact

that its characteristic equality actually holds only for some contexts but not for others. A game of tag or hide-and-go-seek may include children of both sexes and spanning an age range of about seven to twelve; all are equal, and they are likely to experience themselves as such. But when the group is practicing basketball or choosing sides for a baseball or hockey game, the differences in skill associated with age level are likely to become prominent. Age differences of a year or two become significant, and the older boy who can skate faster or catch a ball more reliably becomes a role model for the younger one. Thus, in some contexts, the age differences within the peer group (and associated skill differences) become more significant than the basic age similarity. The younger child sees in the older one a model of what he might become *soon* (while still a child), while the older child becomes aware that he can be a model to younger ones.

A third function of the peer group is that it provides the setting within which the child develops close relationships of his own choosing. Within the larger peer group of equals, children begin about the age of eight and a half to establish special friendships, to find chums.[54] The child begins to construct relationships based on discriminated affinities with others, rather than on simple availability.

The development of friendships within the peer group includes friendships across sex lines. Recent evidence suggests that the once sharply segregated male and female peer groups of preadolescence are gradually giving way. In one study of elementary school children in a small southern city, Broderick and Fowler found that about 20 percent of fifth graders chose someone of the opposite sex as their best friend and more than 50 percent of them chose someone of the opposite sex as one of their four best friends. The authors report that, compared with earlier data, this pattern represents a definite change.[55] They see this as part of a larger pattern of convergence of sex-role expectations and more sharing of values, leading to reduced antagonism between boys and girls, which had been traditional at this age level.

The importance of the peer group in sex education is suggested by further data. For example, in the study just mentioned 65 percent of the fifth graders of both sexes reported having been kissed. Other work cited by Broderick indicates that there is evidently variation from community to community in the rapidity of development of heterosexual activity; he cites some data from a middle-class midwestern city, predominantly Protestant and middle class, in which 50 percent of a sample of 291 boys had engaged in heterosexual play by age eleven, and about 60 percent had done so by age thirteen. More than 20 percent had attempted sexual intercourse by age thirteen.[56] There is evidence to support the view that heterosexual knowledge and activity occur even earlier among lower-class segments of the black community and that the peer group provides the opportunities as well as normative support.[57] However, it must also be said that there has actually been less intensive investigation of peer group sexual practices among white children, both middle class and lower class, than among black lower-class children, so that there is some possibility that apparent differences may be due to the fact that more complete data are available for the latter group.

The subculture of the peer group not only provides a world of standards that is *apart from* that of adults, but it also provides one that is *in opposition to* that of adults. Adults couldn't care less about the proper way to avoid being "it" in a game; they leave that to the children, if they have any awareness of such "problems" at all. But adults often do care about such things as modesty, respect for elders, and other "proprieties," and children often develop corresponding "improprieties." These include ways of talking about subjects that adults frown on and various acts that adults would disapprove of if they knew about them.

Through this distinctive peer culture of childhood and

through the new kinds of relationships that children establish in the peer group, they become more independent of parents and other adult authorities. In the peer group the child develops new emotional ties and identifies with new models. He seeks the attention, acceptance, and good will of peer group members and views himself according to the group's standards. Success in sports, dancing ability, sexual exploits, audacity in provoking adult authority—matters that may be quite unimportant to his family—now become primary considerations in the child's self-image. And as the peer group defines the culture heroes of its time—the football players, the movie stars, the pop singers, the TV performers—the child establishes a solidarity with his generation. When he reaches adulthood and sees his children and *their* peer culture, he becomes aware that his own childhood was passed in a particular time and under historically limited circumstances that make him a member of a particular generation.

The Media of Mass Communication

The media of mass communication comprise newspapers, magazines, comic books, radio, television, movies, and other means of communication that reach large heterogeneous audiences and in which there is an impersonal medium between the sender and receiver.[58] Unlike the other agencies, the mass media do not directly involve interpersonal interaction. Nevertheless, as Donald Horton and R. Richard Wohl point out:

One of the striking characteristics of the new mass media—radio, television, and the movies—is that they give the illusion of face-to-face relationship with the performer. The conditions of response to the performer are analogous to those in a primary group. The most remote and illustrious men are met *as if* they were in the circle of one's peers; the same is true of a character in a story who comes to life in these media in an especially vivid and arresting way. We propose to call this seeming face-to-face relationship between spectator and performer a para-social relationship.

In television, especially, the image which is presented makes available nuances of appearance and gesture to which ordinary social perception is attentive and to which interaction is cued. . . . The audience . . . is . . . subtly insinuated into the program's action and internal social relationships. . . . This simulacrum of conversational give and take may be called para-social interaction.[59]

Since the media include a wide range of materials, they should not be viewed from a single perspective. In content, *The New York Times*, a comedy television show, a soap opera, and a science fiction comic book do not have much in common. Nor can the mass media be considered in isolation. They are ordinarily seen or heard in group settings, and the family and peer group have a considerable influence in guiding exposure to, and generally defining, their content.

Themes and Implications of Mass Media Content

The mass media, by their content alone, teach many of the ways of the society. This is evident in the behavior we take for granted—the duties of the detective, waitress, or sheriff; the functions of the hospital, advertising agency, and police court; behavior in hotel or airplane; the language of the prison, army, or courtroom; the relationship between nurses and doctors or secretaries and their bosses. Such settings and relationships are portrayed time and again in films, television shows, and comic strips; and all "teach"—however misleadingly[60]—norms, status positions, and institutional functions. They provide the child with images of what it might be like to be in such situations and relationships. Until he encounters these situations in actuality, and unless the images are discounted by his significant others, the images serve as his effective "knowledge" of them.

The recurrent themes and story types present values and ideals associated with particular statuses. The Western story form, for example, generally assumes that a law enforcement officer fights for justice and that men who dishonestly seek wealth are evil; the romantic musical implies that love, rather than wealth, makes a girl happy, and that the world of show business is exciting and glamorous.

The mass media also present models of behavior—of heroes, villains, and comics; of occupational, ethnic, and personality types. The models presented by the media wax and wane with the changing times, but certain of their qualities persist through their change of dress. Tarzan has faded, but his agility and courage live on in such successors as Batman, whose mode of levitation is more appropriate to the space age. Although the Western hero still survives as a model of good judgment and self-reliance, he gradually gives way to the detective, the store-front lawyer, and other urban types who take up the twin causes of good character and social order.

Socializing Influence of the Mass Media

The nineteenth-century crusader against vice, Anthony Comstock, began his comprehensive survey of Satan's schemes for victimizing children, *Traps for the Young*, with two chapters on "Household Traps." Among the most sinister of these, in his judgment, was the daily newspaper. An example of how the newspapers do their dirty work of corrupting the young is provided in this account:

The daily papers are turned out by the hundreds of thousands each day, and while ink isn't yet dry the United States mails, the express and railroad companies catch them up, and with almost lightning rapidity scatter them from Maine to California. Into every city, and from every city, this daily stream of printed matter pours, reaching every village, town, hamlet, and almost every home in the land. These publications are mighty educators, either for good or for evil. Sold at a cheap price, from one to five cents each, they are within the reach of all classes. More: they enter the homes—often files of them are preserved—and are especially within the reach of the children, to be read and re-read by them. The father looks over his paper in the morning to ascertain the state of the market, to inform himself as to the news of the day. His attention is attracted by the heavy headlines designed to call especial attention to some disgusting detail of crime. A glance discloses its true character. He turns away in disgust, and thoughtlessly throws down in his library or parlor, within reach of his children, this hateful debauching article, and goes off to business little thinking that what he thus turns from, his child will read with avidity.[61]

Comstock does not tell us whether the home newspaper files were kept by the father in spite of his disgust or whether they were preserved by children who scavenged debauching articles in the parlor after they had been thrown down by the father.

Today, there are commentators who still consider the parlor a scene of debauchery, though the name of the room has been changed to "family room" or "den" and the debaucher is now television instead of the newspaper. According to one study in San Francisco, conducted in the 1950s, 82 percent of children watched TV by the age of five, but none read the newspaper, and only 9 percent had parts of the paper read to them.[62] Furthermore, young readers were introduced to newspapers by their pictorial content rather than by their headlines, and among readers age ten to fifteen, comics were by far the most read items in the paper, followed by news pictures and public affairs cartoons.[63] Such patterns, presumably, persist.

While television may have replaced the newspaper in the minds of critics as a corrupter of the young, the newer and the older view both assume that these media of mass communication can affect the child, and in ways that are considered to impede his preparation for productive membership in adult society. If Comstock's view seems ridiculous today, are his modern-day successors more justified in their concern about the effects of television or comic books?[64]

Before attempting to answer this question, it should be noted that children are exposed to a wide variety of media:

TV, movies, radio, comic books, magazines, and newspapers. Since children begin watching television before they can read and before they go to school, and because children spend many hours watching, even after they have begun school, this medium has been felt to be far more significant in its impact than the other media. It has, accordingly, in recent years attracted the most attention both from critics and social scientists. We shall therefore focus our own attention primarily on television.

Children's Use of Television

Children spend a good deal of time watching television. Although it is difficult to find out just how much time they spend, it has been estimated that the three-year-old who watches television averages forty-five minutes a weekday with the "box," a figure that increases to two hours per weekday at the age of five and rises to a high of about three hours a day somewhere between the fifth and eighth grades.[65] These estimates, based on several studies carried out in various parts of the United States and Canada, indicate some variation by climate and type of location. Viewing tends to be greater in an isolated Rocky Mountain town in winter than in a city with a milder climate such as San Francisco.

During preschool years children's favorite programs tend to be those with animals, cartoon characters, or puppets. During the early school years children's program interests broaden to include not only child-oriented adventure and science fiction but family situation comedies as well.

Socializing Influences of Television

We know, then, that children spend much time watching TV, and we know that they view a variety of kinds of programs, beginning with those that have high animation and proceeding to programs with more talk and people. What effects does watching have on children and how do these effects come about? Is it the content of the programs? the amount of time spent watching? Does television subvert parental influence? school influence? Does it lead them to be antisocial? Does television affect children at all? The questions seem momentous, and the contemporary counterparts of Anthony Comstock have no doubt that television is not merely influential in the lives of children but fundamentally destructive. An assessment of such evidence as is available leads to a somewhat more complex judgment concerning the significance of TV for socialization.

Suppose we begin with the question of whether or not TV subverts parental influence. One survey of the attitudes of 2,500 adults revealed that parents with children under the age of fifteen—both mothers and fathers—were more likely than married people without young children or than single people to believe that children are better off with than without television and that TV's virtues outweigh its drawbacks.[66]

Parents do have objections to TV. They object to certain aspects of the program content—most strongly to the depictions and enactments of violence—but even more strongly they object to the intensity of children's involvement with the medium. Parents complain that it is difficult to get children to do simple things they should do, such as eating meals, helping with housework, or doing school homework.

Yet less than half the parents with children under age fifteen have definite regulations about when and what children can watch. And parents who are fundamentally opposed to television are scarcely more likely to claim regulation of children's viewing than are those who believe children are basically better off with TV.

Despite objections, parents also believe that children learn valuable lessons from TV. Further, parents often admit to using TV as a way of keeping children occupied and thus not doing what parents don't want them to do.

The complexity of parental attitude has been nicely summarized:

So all in all, so far as adult judgments are concerned, television helps to educate the child, but watching it interferes with his education. It helps keep him busy and out of mischief, but it also keeps him too busy to do his chores. It keeps the kids in when you want them, which is good, except for some of the bad things they see. And it keeps them in when you want them out—which is bad even if they see good things. Ideally, then, TV should provide interesting, educational programs that intrigue children when parents don't want to be bothered with them— but not when they ought to be outside doing something else.[67]

If parents are not entirely enchanted with television's effects on their children, believing that watching it deflects children from the proper paths of socialization, they nevertheless find that at times it eases the burdens of their parental responsibilities. Further, parents believe that children learn something from television.

In fact, just about everybody who has anything to say about the matter believes that children learn from television, but the effect of what they learn on their overall socialization is still subject to some uncertainty. To examine this question, we might oversimplify the picture and argue that what children learn from television is (1) good for them and for society, or (2) bad for them and for society, or (3) probably not too significant one way or the other.

Supporting the first view is the argument that television is broadening, that it enlarges children's knowledge of the world. Studies done at a time when television was not yet available in all communities allowed various comparisons between children with and without access to television. The results seem to indicate that children who watch TV begin school with larger vocabularies and greater general knowledge than those who do not, but that this advantage does not last very long once schooling has started.[68] Seventy percent of the elementary school children studied in San Francisco thought television helped them in their school work, particularly in studying current events. Some felt it helped in science. Summarizing a detailed array of research findings, Wilbur Schramm and his co-workers reached these main conclusions: (1) Children probably learn most from television before they learn to read well; (2) both the brightest and the dullest children seem to derive greater learning benefits than children of average intelligence; (3) most of children's learning from television derives from entertainment programs rather than those that are avowedly informational; (4) although television seems to help children get off to "a faster start" in school learning than when TV is not available, the performance gain is only temporary, a result that had also been obtained in an English study.[69]

The second view is based most heavily on the belief that the principal effect of television on children is that it stimulates them to violence. Some journalists and psychiatrists are alarmed that this is the case.[70] Several psychological experiments have shown that children can be stimulated to aggressive feelings and actions by watching TV programs with aggressive content. The implications of these laboratory experiments are evaluated by a distinguished psychologist in these terms:

The implications of these research findings for the impact of television on its viewers are obvious. Given the salience of violence in commercial television, including cartoons especially intended for children, there is every reason to believe that this mass medium is playing a significant role in generating and maintaining a high level of violence in American society, including the nation's children and youth.[71]

The implications are not as unmistakable as this statement declares; and it would be more correct to say that although there is *some* reason to believe this (rather than "every reason"), there is also some reason to doubt it. Even assuming the validity of the evidence that aggressive programs stimulate children to aggressive feelings and actions, to claim a cause-effect relationship between TV violence and "the high level of violence in American society" entails a great analytical leap. An analysis of the causes of violence in society cannot be based on a particular set of childhood experiences but must include consideration of institutions, social strains, and the question of which groups of people are especially prone to what kinds of violence under what kinds of circumstances.

A second reason for doubting a direct connection between the violence on television programs seen by children and the level of violence in American society is that it is by no means clear that the latter is greater than it was in previous periods or than it is in countries where television does not exist or does not feature violent programs. Although it is not certain that there has been an increase in violence in American society, it does seem likely that there has been an increase in the number and articulateness of people who believe that violence can and should be reduced, and this increase may lead to the belief that the amount of violence has increased.[72]

A third reason for skepticism is that much of the research which demonstrates that children are stimulated to aggressive feelings and actions by watching aggressive programs is restricted to that issue. Such research has not sought to investigate other possible effects, although television undoubtedly teaches many lessons, of which violence is but one. To illustrate our meaning, we may consider the cartoon programs that are popular among young children. These programs often show one animal (or human) intent upon harming another. Commonly these attempts fail, as the intended victim repeatedly outwits his would-be assailant. The latter repeatedly devises new stratagems to attain his goal. Now this type of program might teach children to feel aggressive and to behave aggressively after viewing it. But conceivably it might also teach children to maintain their courage or "cool" under attack (by identifying with the clever intended victim) or to maintain determination in the face of repeated frustration (by identifying with the often disappointed would-be assailant). Yet research has not been carried out (or at any rate, has not been published) that investigates, much less weighs, these alternative possibilities. The thematic content of such programs at least suggests the possibility that the main lesson children may learn from them is that resourcefulness *can* prevail over brute force. (Similarly, rather than teaching the satisfactions of violence, Westerns may be teaching that law and order must prevail.) Psychologist Eleanor Maccoby, summarizing some of the literature on the effects of the mass media, notes that it is not yet clear what kinds of behavior are most easily transmitted through observation of characters on a screen, and she concedes the possibility that observing evildoers punished may contribute to the moral education of children.[73]

Although concern with instigation of aggression has been the major basis for considering that what children learn from television is bad for them and society, there have been some others. Lotte Bailyn found that children who spend more time with the mass media (movies and comics as well as television) are more prone to stereotyped thinking.[74] Reviewing this study and others, Maccoby notes inconsistent results among them.[75]

This brings us to the third possibility mentioned above: Perhaps the effects of television are neither as harmful nor as helpful as some have claimed.

Some students of television audiences have noted that children's "involvement with commercials is as deep and intense as it is with programs,"[76] and another notes, "It may be that the commercial message is the most influential aspect of TV."[77] Although few published studies have investigated this aspect of children's involvement with TV, mothers who receive repeated requests from their young children that one advertised item after another be purchased would surely conclude that the most obvious socializing impact of TV is to induct children into the role of consumer in the marketplace. While this may not be the most significant socializing consequence of TV, at this writing it appears the least open to question.

Other Agencies of Socialization

We have discussed the major agencies of socialization; others, too, may be of great significance, depending upon the child and the particular conditions of his life. The church, for example, although less important in modern America than in rural French Canada or early Puritan New England, may still be instrumental in teaching a child to distinguish the sacred from the profane and in instilling feelings of group solidarity. Community agencies, such as Y.M.C.A.s and Boys' Clubs, may have a marked influence, especially insofar as they help widen the outlook of ethnic and lower-class children. Of special importance for many children are athletic teams—some formally organized by adults, such as school teams and the "little leagues" of baseball and hockey, and some informally organized by the children themselves— which may well play an important part in developing values, aspirations, and peer relationships. The summer camp, particularly for middle-class children who attend every year from age three through adolescence, may be important for relationships with both peers and authority figures. Nursery schools and day care centers are growing in number, but the research on their implications for socialization remains inconclusive.[78]

Although specific effects of these agencies remain somewhat elusive, they all function to weaken the child's ties with his family, give him new statuses, teach him different perspectives, and broaden his range of experience.

6 Conclusion: Socialization in Later Life

Socialization continues throughout life. After childhood the person continues to enter new groups, to attain new statuses, to learn new roles and thereby to elaborate his ways of participating in society. A freshman is socialized into the patterns of a college, an immigrant into the life of a new country, a recruit into the army, a new resident into a suburb, a medical student into the profession, a new patient into a hospital ward, and a bride into a life of marriage.

In some respects later socialization is continuous with that of childhood, in other respects discontinuous. The ways in which adult socialization differs from that in childhood will receive our attention later in this chapter. Let us briefly note some continuous aspects. In the home, at school, with the peer group, and through the mass media the child acquires his "native language." He learns to speak and to write. Having developed this foundation in early socialization, he later acquires the capacity to issue commands to an army platoon, to preach sermons, or to write love letters, legal briefs, newspaper articles, or sales reports. He thus learns to use his native language in new and specialized ways, consonant with the particular adult statuses he attains and the expectations of his adult roles. Further, the general symbolic capacities that the child begins to develop in infancy as he begins to acquire his human nature eventuate in his being able also to use special nonverbal symbol systems. He can learn to read music or blueprints—or, for that matter, tea leaves, smoke signals, or tarot cards.

His symbolic capacities are not merely cognitive in nature. These capacities combine with sentiments in particular ways, so that people with whom he has never actually interacted can come to represent aspects of himself. Popes, presidents, and prime ministers can become dear to him as representatives of some ideal or cause that he values. (And so, of course, can other distant figures who do not hold formal office.) This ability to utilize other persons as symbols of oneself (or parts of oneself) and by this means to become attached to large segments of society—church, nation, social movement—does not arise for the first time in adulthood. It is essentially a development from and a refinement of a capacity that first showed itself when the child was attracted to role models outside his family. The child's imagining himself as policeman, heroic rescuer, or football star are the precursors.

Other examples of continuity readily come to mind. In the early games of childhood, the child learns to pursue a goal within a framework of rules. His later ability to play bridge, chess, or tennis is built on his earlier experience with such games as hide-and-seek. The later rules are more elaborate, but the orientation to rules is a refinement of the childhood orientation.

Other basic elements of the adult socialization process are also similar to those in childhood. There are socializing agents who teach, serve as models, and invite participation. Through their ability to offer gratifications and deprivations they induce cooperation and learning, and they endeavor to prevent disruptive deviance. The persons being socialized, on their part, through observation, participation, and role taking, learn and internalize new expectations and develop new self-conceptions.

The continuities in socialization from childhood to adulthood are significant because there is reason to believe that childhood socialization sets limits to what may be accomplished through adult socialization, even though we are not yet able to define those limits with any precision.[2] Nevertheless, there do appear to be limits. The human organism has great plasticity, as we discussed in Chapter 2, but that plasticity is not infinite. For example, it would appear virtually impossible for a person who never learned to read to begin, at age twenty-five, to prepare himself to become a physician. This degree of discontinuity between childhood and adult socialization seems insurmountable.

Although certain aspects and certain kinds of adult socialization presuppose continuity with childhood socialization, it is nevertheless equally true that adult socialization, even in the ordinary course of events, is often discontinuous from that of childhood. Before we turn to these aspects we must say something about the period between childhood and adulthood—adolescence.

Socialization in Adolescence

We cannot do full justice to the literature on adolescence in the brief space available. We shall therefore confine ourselves to a discussion framed generally by this book and this chapter. We shall try to answer this question: Assuming socialization throughout the life cycle to be both continuous and discontinuous, how does adolescence fit into this cycle?

We may begin by noting that the delineation of adolescence as a distinct period of life is not simply derived from observing the biological organism's maturation but is, like childhood, a social invention. Many societies do not identify a distinct period of life as adolescence, and even Western societies did not do so before industrialization. Frank Musgrove goes so far as to claim that

The adolescent was invented at the same time as the steam-engine. The principal architect of the latter was Watt in 1765, of the former Rousseau in 1762. Having invented the adolescent, society has been faced with two major problems: how and where to accommodate him in the social structure, and how to make his behaviour accord with the specifications.[3]

This author further argues that the creation of the concept of adolescence as a distinct period was accompanied by the development of a special psychology of adolescence that largely created its own subject matter. He is claiming that the phenomena associated with adolescence are, in effect, the result of a large self-fulfilling prophecy—that is, because people started believing that there was such a stage of life as adolescence, with distinctive characteristics and problems, and started treating adolescents with such expectations, they elicited the behavior they had come to expect. There seems little doubt that in a general sense Musgrove is substantially correct. If the people we now call teen-agers were still allowed to marry, participate fully and actively in the labor force, and otherwise function as adults instead of being set off as a distinct age group and kept in school, socialization in adolescence would not loom as a topic of discussion. In the American colonies, until the Revolution, fourteen-year-old boys could serve as executors of wills; at sixteen they became men, paying taxes and serving in the militia. Marriages in the middle teens were common. The age at which a young person went to work depended on his family's financial situation and his own physical capacity.[4]

The exclusion of youth from adult employment statuses and roles in the United States was accomplished gradually over the period of about 150 years from the Revolution to the New Deal, and it reflected various social and economic forces. During this period there was increasing awareness of youth as a special age group (whose upper-age limit generally came to be legally defined as eighteen for some purposes, twenty-one for others), and there was a correspondingly increased awareness of "youth problems." Marie Jahoda and Neil Warren report that in 1930, 12 percent of the publications summarized in *Psychological Abstracts* dealt with adolescence, delinquency, and juvenile misbehavior. By 1950 the percentage had risen to 59 percent, and in 1960 to 68 percent.[5] The authors suggest that awareness of adolescent problems has grown concomitantly with the increasing tendency of adolescents to remain in school until graduating from high school, where they remain assembled in a distinctive institution rather than being dispersed in the labor force among people of diverse ages. (As educational aspirations and expectations continue to increase, the period of adolescence tends to be prolonged, so that in the middle class, at least, adolescence is sometimes thought to last until graduation from college. The term "youth" is increasingly used to refer to the age period roughly spanning ages sixteen to twenty-four or so.)[6]

A full treatment of socialization during adolescence merits a volume by itself. Here we shall only delineate in a few broad strokes[7] the central issue of whether adolescent socialization should be regarded as fundamentally continuous or discontinuous with the preceding socialization of childhood and the succeeding socialization of adulthood. The argument for discontinuity has gone through several cycles of enunciation and refutation. In recent times it gained notable support from an influential paper by Talcott Parsons, first published in the early 1940s and widely disseminated during the 1950s as an interest in the sociology of adolescence spread.[8] In this essay Parsons introduced the term "youth culture," whose most notable characteristics he considered to be an emphasis on irresponsibility and pleasure seeking—exemplified by concern with "having a good time," heterosocial activities, and athletics—which he contrasted with the emphasis on responsibility in adulthood. Evidence that this emphasis on discontinuity was exaggerated has been presented by Frederick Elkin and William Westley.[9]

The argument in favor of discontinuity was reinvigorated during the 1960s with the publication of a study by James S. Coleman of ten widely varying high schools in Illinois.[10] Coleman starts with the assumption that adolescents constitute a small society of their own, one that "maintains only a few threads of connection with the outside adult society." He does not examine the quantity or the nature of the "threads of connection," even though much of his argument is built upon this assumption. By means of questionnaires administered to the several thousand boys and girls in these high schools, Coleman found that they placed much greater value on athletics and popularity than on academic performance and that intellectual values generally had little to do with popularity among peers (although there were variations among schools in the importance attributed to scholarship by the students). He found further evidence of the "irresponsibility" pattern noted by Parsons—for example, great interest in cars (and activities and paraphernalia related to cars). He found, in effect, that adolescents are socialized into a subculture, a special society of their own peers and dominated by their own values. And since the schools are identified by Coleman as society's established agency for preparing adolescents to participate in the adult world, he argues that the activities and values of adolescents are discontinuous with, and in opposition to, the world of adults.

Coleman acknowledges that what constitutes a subculture depends partly upon definition. But despite numerous qualifications that he makes in the course of reporting many data, his basic position is quite clear.

Although there is no doubt that adolescents are in the process of becoming more independent of their parents and, consequently, are more responsive to their peers than they were at younger ages, and although their interests and values may differ from those ostensibly emphasized by the high school, it does not follow that adolescent socialization is peer-dominated and little influenced by adult values and norms. In reviewing Coleman's study, Bennett Berger argues that most of the adolescent values and interests noted by Coleman are more accurately understood as derivative from adults. For example, high school athletics depend greatly on support by parents and local booster organizations. Further, parents are concerned about popularity and prestige. Emphasizing the continuity of adolescent and adult values, Berger comments, "From Coleman's treatment of the *adolescent* 'subculture' one might think that cars and masculine prowess and feminine glamour and social activities and sex and dating and wearing the right clothes and being from the right family were concerns entirely alien to American adults."[11] He points out that athletics, extracurricular activities, and social affairs are sponsored by the schools and are considered to be training grounds for adult responsibilities. Berger thus argues, with some cogency we believe, that Coleman's data tend to support conclusions nearly opposite from those Coleman himself draws from them and that much of what takes place during adolescence may be regarded as *anticipatory socialization* for adulthood, rather than as evidence for a discontinuous interval. (The concept of anticipatory socialization refers to the rehearsal of feelings, values, and actions that takes place before a person actually enters upon a particular status or adopts a new role.)

In contrast to Coleman's emphasis on the separateness of the adolescent from adult society, Edgar Friedenberg is impressed by the extent of adult control, precisely in the high schools. In a study of nine high schools he found that the first social lesson adolescents learn is that they are subject to compulsory attendance and various other specialized regulations (such as requiring a corridor pass to walk through the halls). Such restrictions, he suggests, teach them—although admittedly some steps are skipped in the analysis

—that "they do not participate fully in the freedoms guaranteed by the state, and that, *therefore, these freedoms do not really partake of the character of inalienable rights.*"[12] Friedenberg and Coleman thus both argue that adolescent socialization is not a proper preparation for adulthood; but whereas Coleman finds the cause in the adolescent society, Friedenberg finds it in the restrictive authority system of the high school. Indeed, Friedenberg argues that adolescents are being pressed prematurely into adulthood.[13] Friedenberg and Berger thus agree that adolescence is quite directly preparatory for adulthood—perhaps more directly than it should be.

In summary, as Marie Jahoda and Neil Warren have pointed out,[14] one can find evidence to "prove" the existence of a youth culture, if one wishes; or one can likewise find evidence to bear out the contention that the fundamental fact of adolescent socialization is its continuity with and preparation for adulthood. The argument depends on the groups studied, the data selected, and the conceptual approach adopted.

In our own view, the evidence to date suggests that, with regard to fundamental values, the continuity of adolescent socialization with adulthood outweighs the discontinuity. Adolescent values and behavior have been more reflective of adult values and behavior than either Parsons or Coleman believe to be the case. But today the situation *seems* more in flux than before. It may be, as Margaret Mead argues, that we are on the threshold of a new and unprecedented era— one in which the traditional direction of socialization will be reversed and the young will begin to socialize their elders, because the young will have the most relevant information and ideas about the world as it is coming to be.[15] Whether such an era actually comes to pass remains to be seen.[16]

Socialization in Adulthood

There are several reasons why socialization does not terminate with childhood or even adolescence. One is that the person enters into new statuses with new role expectations when he reaches adulthood and he must learn how to function in them. His earlier socialization gives him some preparation, but much of what he needs to know can only be learned when he is actually in his new situation. Thus, boys and girls receive considerable anticipatory socialization for marriage throughout their lives prior to marriage—by observing their own parents and other married couples, by talking about it with their peers, by vicariously experiencing various kinds of marriages portrayed in the mass media. But it is only when they are actually in the new status and role and have made a *commitment* to marriage that they both need and wish to change themselves to function as actual married partners.[17]

A second reason is that many groups, statuses, and roles become known to a person only after he has reached adulthood. This is particularly evident with regard to occupations. Only a relatively small number of occupations are known to children and young adolescents. As we noted earlier, the mass media portray a much smaller array of occupations than exists in the actual world,[18] and this picture is only moderately amplified through the child's personal acquaintance and school learning.

A third reason is that the person continues in adulthood to encounter people who become for him new significant others. Some of them may be his own peers; others may be senior to him in age or social status or both; they may even be his own children. Through encounters he may learn to value skiing, or drug taking, or working in community endeavors, or playing the stock market—or any combination of these or other activities.

Encounters with new significant others may occur in various ways. The mass media of communication provide one avenue. For example, during the 1960s John F. Kennedy was widely believed to have stimulated heightened interest in politics, and many of those attracted to him were undoubtedly reached through the media, especially television. During the 1930s and 1940s, the era of "big stars," film actresses became significant others to many moviegoers, who copied their hair styles and in other ways sought to model themselves after one or another "glamour girl." Indeed, the concept of "glamour" gained currency as a value in living via the films and the array of magazines devoted to accounts of film stars and their doings.

New significant others can be neighbors as well as distant figures. Moving into a new suburb results in new patterns of informal interaction, and new neighbors become important to each other as sources of mutual expectations.[19] The role of neighbor itself may have to be learned anew, especially for the person who previously lived in a big-city apartment and now becomes a homeowner. A norm of casual accessibility, rather than a norm of determined insularity, is likely to govern, and this may entail willingness to borrow and lend (lawn mowers and cups of sugar), as well as routine forms of cooperation such as participating in a car pool.

One major consideration underlying all the reasons cited for the continuing importance of socialization in adult life is the fact that both maturation and previous socialization present new demands and new opportunities to the person. Generally speaking, childhood socialization endows the child with the capacities for participating in adult society in *some* ways. Adult socialization makes possible his participation in *specific* ways, through participation in particular institutions of society. Following Erik Erikson, we may say that the period through adolescence ordinarily results in the establishment of the person's core identity. Although his identity will be further developed and modified (and, in certain extreme situations such as battlefield fighting, imprisonment, religious conversion, or hospitalization for mental illness, drastically altered), the establishment of a core identity provides the person with a kind of platform from which he may *launch himself* into further socialization. The importance of the establishment of a core identity is that it provides the person with the opportunities and the capacities for *choice*, and this is one of the fundamental distinctions between child and adult socialization (recognizing, of course, that external circumstance conditions choice). With his biological sexual maturity, the person may choose to lead a celibate or active sexual life. He may choose to marry or to remain single or to live in a commune; to become a parent or not, to have few children or many. He may choose to pursue a college education or go to work as soon as he can find a job. When he goes to work, he may seek to work for a large bureaucratic enterprise or a smaller more personal organization; or he may remain relatively independent, as a taxi driver, traveling salesman, lawyer, or physician. With all such choices, the person is also choosing environments in which he will be further socialized, although he will have no more than a vague idea of what his later socialization experiences will be until he is actually enacting the choices he has made and interacting with others whose choices have brought them into contact with him.

The Nature of Adult Socialization

At the beginning of this chapter we discussed certain ways in which adult socialization is continuous with childhood socialization. Now we ask: How do they differ? Irving Rosow provides one answer. He begins by observing that socialization involves the effort to inculcate both values and behavior so that "the fully socialized person internalizes the correct beliefs and displays the appropriate behavior." But socialization is not always fully successful. Four different types of people can be identified by asking whether they adopt both the values and behavior to which they are being socialized, neither, or one or the other. The socialized are those who adopt both, the unsocialized those who adopt neither. In between are the "dilettante," who adopts the values but not the behavior, and the "chameleon," who displays the expected behavior but does not subscribe to the values. The most suggestive distinction Rosow makes is between the socialized and the chameleon, since both are similar in behavior but different in their commitment to values. Rosow contends that the chameleon type of outcome to socialization is found in many different relationships:

> . . . the stereotyped complaisance of many Negroes in traditional contacts with whites, in the orientation of prostitutes to clients, in the involuntary union member in a closed shop, in the married homosexual, in the unskilled worker in the marginal labor market who has no occupational or organizational identity but fits tolerably into a diversity of work situations. It is also familiar in the typical adjustment of most draftees to military life, in the adaptation of lower ranks of large-scale organizations . . .[20]

He then goes on to argue that "chameleon conformity may be the most common pattern in complex societies." In this view, full socialization is concentrated in a few areas of a person's life. Since any given person is not fully committed to the various positions he occupies and the groups to which he belongs, his socialization type will differ with each of them, so that he is "a chameleon in one, a dilettante in a second, and fully socialized in a third."

Orville Brim picks up Rosow's analysis and carries it further by stating that the most important change from socialization in childhood to that in adulthood is a shift from emphasis on values and motives to emphasis on overt behavior.[21] Brim also points out other significant differences:

1. "Synthesis of old material" rather than acquisition of new material
2. A shift from an idealistic to a realistic outlook
3. Learning how to handle conflicting demands
4. Socialization for increasingly specific roles[22]

The Contexts of Adult Socialization

Important aspects of adult socialization take place in formally organized settings such as colleges and trade schools, work organizations, professional associations, and the military services. There are also special settings—such as prisons and mental hospitals—for those whose earlier socialization comes to be adjudged so seriously faulty that their behavior is deemed to fall outside the range of socially accepted outcomes of socialization. (In Rosow's terms, they are not good chameleons, although some might be dilettantes.)

Stanton Wheeler has attempted to identify some of the main features of these adult socialization settings, features more or less common to all of them, regardless of type.[23] He also notes some important differences between "developmental" socialization organizations as a type (schools, colleges, work organizations) and "resocialization" organizations (prisons, mental hospitals). The latter merit more extended treatment than can be given them here; we shall therefore consider only the developmental organizations, which ordinarily result in socially acceptable socialization outcomes. Although some aspects of Wheeler's analysis may also apply to such childhood settings as the school, our focus here is on adult socialization and on the aspects of organizations that affect socialization outcomes.

The person who enters an organization may be designated a *recruit*. The organization has goals of its own that lead to its providing goals to the recruit. When these are specific goals, such as teaching typing or engineering, the organization is concerned with role socialization. When they are general, such as teaching liberal arts, the concern is with status socialization—preparing the recruit to occupy a generalized status in life and to enact an associated life style. Some organizations may be concerned with both types of goals.[24]

Recruits move through an organization in a sequence of steps. Organizations that have great control over entry procedures may be able to provide an adequate period of anticipatory socialization. Even so, recruits often experience "reality shock" upon entry—what they had anticipated was either misleading or seriously incomplete. The situation in which they find themselves is unexpected—as when the college freshman is jolted by the amount of work he is expected to do or the graduate of the secretarial school, expecting to be an executive secretary, is assigned routine filing.

Usually, there are entry procedures of some kind, in which information is exchanged. The recruits receive "an orientation" and learn somewhat more definitely what is expected of them. The socializing agents, in turn, form initial impressions of the recruits and therefore anticipations of what may be expected from them in the way of performance. Of course, other information about the recruits may have been acquired earlier, information from application forms, tests, letters of recommendation, interviews, and transcripts of school grades.

Organizations generally have definite expectations concerning the length of time the recruit is expected to stay in the socialization program. After that time he goes through specified exit procedures: graduation from college, assignment to independent responsibilities in a work organization, qualifying examinations for such professions as law or medicine.

The socialization process in formal organizations is not governed entirely by the organization and its officially designated agents. Recruits respond to the situations presented to them and often develop their own norms. An illustration of this is provided in a study of medical students by Howard S. Becker and his associates.[25] Freshman medical students, they found, enter with the expectation of learning everything that is taught them. In the course of the first few weeks they begin to feel overloaded and realize they have set themselves an almost impossible task, so they shift their perspective to trying to learn "only the things that are important." Before the first year is over, the emphasis has shifted to learning what the students think the faculty wants them to know and will ask about on examinations. Student and faculty perspectives differ as to what students should learn and how to judge how much they have learned.

Wilbert Moore has noted that punishment—in the form of heavy work load, great isolation, or required performance of unpleasant tasks and duties—is a component in all socialization to occupations that have high standards of competence and performance and that exhibit high identification of members with the collectivity of fellow practitioners.[26]

All adult socialization leads to some changes in self-image. The formation of a specific occupational identity results, Moore suggests, from these main factors:

1. Learning the language and skills of an occupation
2. Surviving the ordeals that have punished the recruit and his fellows
3. Accepting fellow recruits and adult role models as significant others for oneself
4. Internalizing the occupational norms, so that self-respect becomes a powerful constraint on poor performance or violation of standards
5. Continuing to be aware of peers as purveyors of potential sanctions
6. Being aware of formal reinforcements, the most important of which is the lack of a market for the services of poor performers

This is, of course, again in Rosow's terms, a model of full socialization; it does not throw much light on how dilettantes and chameleons are produced or on the fact that some of them even do quite well in the market. Questions raised by such observations, however, have not yet been studied carefully.

Socialization for Growing Old

It is now recognized in sociology and other social sciences that socialization is a lifelong activity. In recent years a new discipline has developed—gerontology—concerned with the basic question: What is aging? The long-accepted answer had been that it was basically a biological process with some secondary psychological aspects ("You're as young as you feel"). Increasingly, however, investigators are asking whether there may not be self-fulfilling prophecies built into the process.

According to one theory, aging individuals are motivated naturally to disengage from and relinquish the active roles for which they have been socialized in earlier life;[27] but Matilda Riley and her associates provide evidence to justify questioning this view. They suggest that the aging individual does not seek disengagement from social participation; rather, society operates in many ways to withdraw roles from the aging individual, roles that he might well wish to continue. He is socialized to accept the withdrawal of roles. This is most easily shown with regard to work roles. Retirement is formally defined in many organizations as occurring at a certain age. The individual is expected to retire at that age and is socialized to define his leaving work as retirement (though other norms might define it as discriminatory exclusion from the labor market). There is anticipatory socialization for retirement: The person's "work role deteriorates around him." He may be by-passed for promotion or barred from retraining programs available to younger workers. Performance expectations may rise to levels unattainable by the older worker, resulting in subtle depreciation of his performance.

On the basis of scattered evidence, Riley and coauthors suggest that older people, if healthy and provided with useful social roles, might not withdraw. They note that under present conditions "widespread withdrawal might be entirely predictable from the *social* structure—quite apart from any organic or personality changes in the aging *individual*."[28]

As society changes, more and more life situations formerly left to chance and to individual adjustment are coming to be defined as situations for which the person should be formally

socialized. The replacement of apprenticeship by more formalized training programs for work has long been accepted.
Increasingly, marriage and parenthood themselves are
thought to require formal socialization.[29] And more recently,
with more and more people living to advanced age, the need
for education for retirement from mature social roles has
become a common cry. In modern industrial societies the
concern with the outcomes of socialization does not abate.

Notes
and References

Chapter 2. Preconditions for Socialization

1. Charles Horton Cooley, *Social Organization* (New York: Scribner, 1909), p. 27.
2. *Ibid.*, p. 30.
3. Kingsley Davis, "Final Note on a Case of Extreme Isolation," *American Journal of Sociology*, 52 (1947), 432–437.
4. J. A. L. Singh and Robert M. Zingg, *Wolf Children and Feral Man* (New York: Harper, 1939).
5. Bruno Bettelheim, "Feral Children and Autistic Children," *American Journal of Sociology*, 64 (1959), 455–467.
6. René A. Spitz, "Hospitalism," *The Psychoanalytic Study of the Child*, 1 (1945), 53–72; and "Hospitalism: A Follow-Up Report," *ibid.*, 2 (1946), 113–117.
7. H. F. Harlow, M. K. Harlow, R. O. Dodsworth, and G. L. Arling, "Maternal Behavior of Rhesus Monkeys Deprived of Mothering and Peer Associations in Infancy," *Proceedings of the American Philosophical Society*, 110 (February 1966), 58–66; Bill Seay and Harry F. Harlow, "Maternal Separation in the Rhesus Monkey," *Journal of Nervous and Mental Disease*, 140 (1965), 434–441; Harry F. Harlow, "Primary Affectional Patterns in Primates," *American Journal of Orthopsychiatry*, 30 (1960), 676–684; M. K. Harlow, "Affection in Primates," *Discovery* (January 1966).

8. S. J. Freedman, H. U. Grunebaum, M. Greenblatt, "Perceptual and Cognitive Changes in Sensory Deprivation," in Philip Solomon et al. (eds.), *Sensory Deprivation* (Cambridge, Mass.: Harvard University Press, 1965), p. 69.

Chapter 3. The Processes of Socialization

1. Alex Inkeles, "Society, Social Structure and Child Socialization," in John A. Clausen (ed.), *Socialization and Society* (Boston: Little, Brown, 1968).
2. M. Brewster Smith, "Competence and Socialization," *ibid.*
3. Inkeles, *op. cit.*, pp. 87–88. Copyright © 1968 by Little, Brown and Company (Inc.). Reprinted by permission.
4. The evidence on nutrition and learning is evaluated in Herbert G. Birch, M.D., and Joan Dye Gussow, *Disadvantaged Children: Health, Nutrition and School Failure* (New York: Harcourt, Brace/Grune & Stratton, 1970). See also Nevin S. Scrimshaw and J .E. Gordon (eds.), *Malnutrition, Learning and Behavior* (Cambridge, Mass.: M.I.T. Press, 1968).
5. W. Lloyd Warner, Robert J. Havighurst, Martin B. Loeb, *Who Shall Be Educated?* (New York: Harper and Brothers, 1944).
6. Bruno Bettelheim, *Symbolic Wounds: Puberty Rites and the Envious Male* (New York: Free Press, 1954).
7. Norton T. Dodge, *Women in the Soviet Economy* (Baltimore: Johns Hopkins Press, 1966), pp. 208 and 210.
8. Charles Winick, *The New People: Desexualization in American Life* (New York: Pegasus, 1968).
9. The concept of the infant as evocative is discussed in Gerald Handel, "Analysis of Correlative Meaning: The TAT in the Study of Whole Families," in Gerald Handel (ed.), *The Psychosocial Interior of the Family* (Chicago: Aldine, 1967; London: G. Allen & Unwin, 1968), pp. 104–106.
10. Bettye M. Caldwell, "The Effects of Infant Care," in Martin L. Hoffman and Lois Wladis Hoffman (eds.), *Review of Child Development Research*, Vol. 1 (New York: Russell Sage Foundation, 1964). Contemporary psychoanalytic views are presented in E. James Anthony and Therese Benedek (eds.), *Parenthood: Its Psychology and Psychopathology* (Boston: Little, Brown, 1970).
11. Lois B. Murphy, *The Widening World of Childhood* (New York: Basic Books, 1962), cited in Caldwell, *op. cit.*
12. Leon J. Yarrow, "Separation from Parents During Early Childhood," in Hoffman and Hoffman, *op. cit.*, p. 98.
13. M. Ainsworth, "The Development of Infant-Mother Interaction Among the Ganda," in B. M. Foss (ed.), *Determinants of Infant Behavior II* (New York: Wiley, 1963), cited in Yarrow, *op. cit.*

14. Some examples of the different ways in which the infant's cry is symbolically interpreted by mothers are reported in the section "Leaving the Baby to Cry" in John and Elizabeth Newson, *Infant Care in an Urban Community* (London: George Allen & Unwin; New York: International Universities Press, 1963), Chapter 6, "The Roots of Socialization," pp. 87–99.

15. An overview of recent work is given in James J. Jenkins, "The Acquisition of Language," in David A. Goslin (ed.), *Handbook of Socialization Theory and Research* (Chicago: Rand McNally, 1969), Chapter 13.

16. This account of the work of these linguistic scholars is adapted from Jenkins, *op. cit.*

17. *Ibid.*, p. 675.

18. *Ibid.*, p. 679.

19. Sigmund Freud, "Three Contributions to the Theory of Sex," in A. A. Brill (ed.), *The Basic Writings of Sigmund Freud*, Book III (New York: Modern Library, 1938), p. 581.

20. Ernest G. Schachtel, *Metamorphosis* (New York: Basic Books, 1959), Chapter 12, "On Memory and Childhood Amnesia," pp. 287–289. Reprinted by permission.

21. Mead does not himself use these examples. His most influential work is presented in George H. Mead, *Mind, Self and Society* (Chicago: University of Chicago Press, 1934). Interpretation and elaboration of his work are found in Herbert Blumer, *Symbolic Interactionism* (Englewood Cliffs, N.J.: Prentice-Hall, 1969); Jerome Manis and Bernard Meltzer (eds.), *Symbolic Interaction* (Boston: Allyn and Bacon, 1967); and Arnold M. Rose (ed.), *Human Behavior and Social Processes, An Interactionist Approach* (Boston: Houghton Mifflin, 1962).

22. Mead, *op. cit.*, p. 151.

23. Mead, *op. cit.*, p. 155.

24. Philippe Ariès, *Centuries of Childhood* (New York: Knopf, 1962), pp. 128 and 411. Reprinted by permission.

25. *Ibid.*, pp. 176–177.

26. The following summary of Erikson's approach is adapted from two of his works, *Childhood and Society* (New York: Norton, 1950) and *Identity: Youth and Crisis* (New York: Norton, 1968).

27. Erikson, *Identity: Youth and Crisis*, p. 124. This and the following quotations from the same work are reprinted by permission of W. W. Norton and Faber and Faber Ltd.

28. Erikson, *ibid.*, p. 132.

29. Erikson, *Childhood and Society*, p. 231.

30. Alice S. Rossi, "Transition to Parenthood," *Journal of Marriage and Family*, 30 (February 1968), 26–39.

31. Erikson, *Identity: Youth and Crisis*, p. 139.

32. Erikson, *Childhood and Society*, Chapter 3, "Hunters Across the Prairie."

33. Albert J. Reiss, "Social Organization and Socialization: Varia-

tions on a Theme about Generations," unpublished paper (1965), cited in Eleanor E. Maccoby, "The Development of Moral Values and Behavior in Childhood," in John A. Clausen (ed.), op. cit.

34. Erikson, Identity: Youth and Crisis, pp. 257–258.

Chapter 4. Socialization and Subcultural Patterns

1. Margaret Mead, in Margaret Mead and Martha Wolfenstein (eds.), Childhood in Contemporary Cultures (Chicago: University of Chicago Press, 1955), Chapter 1, p. 10. Copyright 1955 by The University of Chicago. © The University of Chicago, 1955. Reprinted by permission.

2. The idea of different cultures is most strongly embodied in Oscar Lewis's notion of a "culture of poverty." This and related ideas are discussed and challenged in a carefully reasoned work by Charles A. Valentine, Culture and Poverty: Critique and Counter-Proposals (Chicago: University of Chicago Press, 1968).

3. Valentine, ibid., p. 106.

4. Anne Moody, Coming of Age in Mississippi, An Autobiography (New York: Delta, 1970), p. 23.

5. See, for example, Arthur J. Vidich and Joseph Bensman, Small Town in Mass Society (Princeton, N. J.: Princeton University Press, enlarged edition, 1969).

6. William Graham Sumner, Folkways (Boston: Ginn, 1906), p. 13.

7. Tamotsu Shibutani and Kian M. Kwan, Ethnic Stratification (New York: Macmillan, 1965), p. 109.

8. Writings that exemplify this belief include Nelson N. Foote and Leonard S. Cottrell, Jr., Identity and Interpersonal Competence (Chicago: University of Chicago Press, 1955); Ronald Lippitt, "Improving the Socialization Process," in John A. Clausen (ed.), Socialization and Society (Boston: Little, Brown, 1968); and Eugene A. Weinstein, "The Development of Interpersonal Competence," in David A. Goslin (ed.), Handbook of Socialization Theory and Research (Chicago: Rand McNally, 1969).

9. Celia Stendler, Children of Brasstown (Urbana: University of Illinois Press, 1949).

10. Bernice Neugarten, in W. Lloyd Warner et al., Democracy in Jonesville (New York: Harper, 1949), Chapter 5.

11. Hyman Rodman, "The Lower-Class Value Stretch," Social Forces, 42 (December 1963), p. 205.

12. Melvin J. Kohn, "Social Class and Parent-Child Relationships: An Interpretation," American Journal of Sociology, 68 (January 1963), 471–480.

13. Robert D. Hess and Gerald Handel, Family Worlds (Chicago: University of Chicago Press, 1959), Chapter 5, p. 174.

14. John R. Seeley, R. A. Sim, and E. W. Looseley, Crestwood

Heights: A Study of the Culture of Suburban Life (New York: Basic Books, 1956; paperback edition, New York. Wiley, 1963), p. 470.

15. *Ibid.*, p. 306.
16. Kohn, *op. cit.*; Leonard I. Pearlin and Melvin L. Kohn, "Social Class, Occupation, and Parental Values: A Cross-National Study," *American Sociological Review*, 31 (August 1966), 466–479, reprinted in Alan L. Grey (ed.), *Class and Personality in Society* (New York: Atherton Press, 1969).
17. Kohn, *op. cit.*; Lee Rainwater, Richard P. Coleman, and Gerald Handel, *Workingman's Wife: Her Personality, World and Life Style* (New York: Oceana Publications, 1959; paperback, Macfadden Books, 1962).
18. Basil Bernstein, "Social Class and Linguistic Development: A Theory of Social Learning," in A. H. Halsey, Jean Floud, and C. Arnold Anderson (eds.), *Education, Economy and Society* (New York: Free Press, 1961), pp. 288–314.
19. Robert D. Hess, Virginia Shipman, and David Jackson, "Early Experience and the Socialization of Cognitive Modes in Children," *Child Development*, 36 (December 1965), 869–886.
20. Louis Schneider and Sverre Lysgaard, "The Deferred Gratification Pattern: A Preliminary Study," *American Sociological Review*, 18 (April 1953), 142–149, reprinted in Alan Grey, *op. cit.*
21. S. M. Miller and Frank Riessman, "The Working Class Subculture: A New View," *Social Problems*, 9 (1961), 86–97; reprinted in Alan Grey, *op. cit.*
22. Allison Davis, "Socialization and Adolescent Personality," *Adolescence, Forty-Third Yearbook*, Part I (Chicago: National Society for the Study of Education, 1944), Chapter II.
23. Albert K. Cohen and Harold M. Hodges, Jr., "Characteristics of the Lower-Blue-Collar-Class," *Social Problems*, 10 (Spring 1963), 303–334. Our account of lower-class subculture draws mainly on this article, unless otherwise indicated.
24. Cohen and Hodges, *op. cit.*, p. 322.
25. Eleanor Pavenstadt, "A Comparison of the Child-Rearing Environment of Upper Lower and Very Lower Class Families," *American Journal of Orthopsychiatry*, 35 (January 1965), 89–98. The quotation is taken from the summary given in Bernard Goldstein, *Low Income Youth in Urban Areas. A Critical Review of the Literature.* (New York: Holt, Rinehart and Winston, 1967), p. 11. Reprinted by permission.
26. Luther P. Jackson, "Telling It Like It Is!" (Washington: Health and Welfare Council of the Capital Area, 1966), quoted in Elizabeth Herzog, *About the Poor: Some Facts and Some Fictions* (Washington: U.S. Department of Health, Education and Welfare, 1968), Chapter 1, "Problem Populations: 'They' and 'We.'"
27. For example, Kurt Mayer and Walter Buckley, *Class and Society* (New York: Random House, 1970); Bennett M. Berger, *Working*

Class Suburb (Berkeley: University of California Press, 1960); Herbert J. Gans, *The Urban Villagers: Group and Class in the Life of Italian-Americans* (New York: Free Press, 1962); Arthur Shostak, *Blue-Collar Life* (New York: Random House, 1969); William M. Dobriner, *Class in Suburbia* (Englewood Cliffs, N. J.: Prentice-Hall, 1963); C. Wright Mills, *White Collar: The American Middle Classes* (New York: Oxford University Press, 1951); Charles H. Page, *Class and American Society* (New York: Schocken, 1969).

28. The account that follows is adapted from Harry M. Caudill, *Night Comes to the Cumberlands: A Biography of a Depressed Area* (Boston: Little, Brown, 1962).

29. *Ibid.*, p. 51.

30. *Ibid.*, p. 146.

31. *Ibid.*, pp. 337–338.

32. Richard A. Ball, "A Poverty Case: The Analgesic Subculture of the Southern Appalachians," *American Sociological Review*, 33 (December 1968), 885–895.

33. Jack E. Weller, *Yesterday's People: Life in Contemporary Appalachia* (Lexington: University of Kentucky Press, 1965), pp. 47–48. Reprinted by permission.

34. Gunnar Myrdal, *An American Dilemma* (New York: Harper and Brothers, 1944), p. 157.

35. Shibutani and Kwan, *op. cit.*, p. 47.

36. *Ibid.*, p. 470.

37. Mary Ellen Goodman, *Race Awareness in Young Children* (Cambridge: Addison-Wesley, 1952).

38. Marian Radke Yarrow, "Personality Development and Minority Group Membership," in Marshall Sklare (ed.), *The Jews: Social Patterns of an American Group* (New York: Free Press, 1958).

39. The suggestion has been made that *generation* is a less useful concept than *cohort*, which is defined as "the aggregate of individuals (within some population definition) who experienced the same event within the same time interval." See Norman B. Ryder, "The Cohort As a Concept in the Study of Social Change," *American Sociological Review*, 30 (December 1965), 843–861. The implication of this approach in the present context would be that children of immigrants ("second generation") in, say, 1880 had different socialization experiences from children of immigrants in 1970. Although this is undoubtedly true, it does not mean that the fact of being second-generation may not have common features regardless of the time at which it occurs. For our purposes here, the notion of "generation" remains useful.

40. Elena Padilla, *Up From Puerto Rico* (New York: Columbia University Press, 1958), p. 31.

41. The nature of slums is discussed in Part I of Marshall B. Clinard, *Slums and Community Development* (New York: Free Press, 1966); and by F. William Howton, "Cities, Slums and Accultura-

tive Process in Developing Countries," in Milton C. Albrecht (ed.), *Studies in Sociology*, Buffalo Studies (Buffalo: State University of New York at Buffalo, 1967).

42. Hylan Lewis, Foreword to Elliot Liebow, *Tally's Corner: A Study of Negro Streetcorner Men* (Boston: Little, Brown, 1967), pp. vii–viii. Reprinted by permission.

43. Toshio Yatsushiro, "The Japanese Americans," in Milton L. Barron (ed.), *American Minorities* (New York: Knopf, 1957), pp. 322–323.

44. Reported in Beatrice Griffith, *American Me* (Boston: Houghton Mifflin, 1948), p. 151.

45. Robert K. Merton, *Social Theory and Social Structure* (New York: Free Press, 1968), pp. 281 ff.

46. Shibutani and Kwan, *op. cit.*, p. 357.

47. Fred L. Strodtbeck, "Family Interaction, Values, and Achievement," in Sklare, *op. cit.*, p. 149.

48. Bernard C. Rosen, "Race, Ethnicity, and the Achievement Syndrome," *American Sociological Review*, 24 (1959), 47–60.

49. Nathan Glazer and Daniel Patrick Moynihan, *Beyond the Melting Pot: The Negroes, Puerto Ricans, Jews, Italians and Irish of New York City*, 2nd ed. (Cambridge: M.I.T. Press, 1970), p. 310.

50. *Ibid.* The two editions are virtually identical except for the addition of a new introduction to the second edition. Compare the discussion of religion and ethnicity on pp. xxxi ff. with that on pp. 313 ff.

Chapter 5. Agencies of Socialization

1. David Riesman, with Reuel Denny and Nathan Glazer, *The Lonely Crowd: A Study of the Changing American Character* (New Haven: Yale University Press, 1950).

2. Robert K. Merton, *Social Theory and Social Structure* (New York: Free Press, 1968), enlarged edition, chapter entitled "Manifest and Latent Functions."

3. Allen Kassof, *The Soviet Youth Program: Regimentation and Rebellion* (Cambridge, Mass.: Harvard University Press, 1965), p. 173.

4. Dennis Wrong, "The Oversocialized Conception of Man in Modern Sociology," *American Sociological Review*, 26 (April 1961), 183–193. An enlarged version of this article is printed in *Psychoanalysis and the Psychoanalytic Review*, 49 (Summer 1962), where it is accompanied by a rebuttal from Talcott Parsons entitled "Individual Autonomy and Social Pressure: An Answer to Dennis H. Wrong," pp. 70–79.

5. Jean Evans, *Three Men* (New York: Knopf, 1950), p. 11.

6. Peter Blau and Otis D. Duncan, *The American Occupational Structure* (New York: Wiley, 1967), p. 330.

7. Elaboration of the family's mediating role is presented in Gerald Handel (ed.), *The Psychosocial Interior of the Family* (Chicago: Aldine, 1967), Part III, "The Family as Mediator of the Culture."

8. David A. Schulz, *Coming Up Black: Patterns of Ghetto Socialization* (Englewood Cliffs, N. J.: Prentice-Hall, 1969).

9. This analysis is developed by Lee Rainwater, "Crucible of Identity: The Negro Lower-Class Family," *Daedalus, Journal of the American Academy of Arts and Sciences*, 95 (1966), 172–216.

10. Handel, *op. cit.*; Robert D. Hess and Gerald Handel, *Family Worlds* (Chicago: University of Chicago Press, 1959).

11. In one study Harris found that both mothers and fathers "invariably showed evidence of using their parenthood to continue or to resolve, through their children, some aspects of their own growing up, and therefore each of their several children might represent a somewhat different aspect of their past." Irving Harris, *Normal Children and Mothers* (New York: Free Press, 1959), p. 39.

12. Talcott Parsons and Robert F. Bales, *Family, Socialization and Interaction Process* (Glencoe, Ill.: Free Press, 1955), Chapter II, "Family Structure and the Socialization of the Child."

13. Herbert J. Gans, *The Urban Villagers: Group and Class in the Life of Italian-Americans* (New York: Free Press, 1962), pp. 54, 59–60. Italics in original.

14. Jack E. Weller, *Yesterday's People: Life in Contemporary Appalachia* (Lexington: University of Kentucky Press, 1965).

15. Norman W. Bell, "Extended Family Relations of Disturbed and Well Families," *Family Process*, 1 (September 1962), 175–193.

16. Leonard Benson, *Fatherhood: A Sociological Perspective* (New York: Random House, 1968), p. 3.

17. Talcott Parsons, *Social Structure and Personality* (New York: Free Press, 1964), Chapter 2, "The Father Symbol: An Appraisal in the Light of Psychoanalytic and Sociological Theory." Our account is a necessarily oversimplified version of Parsons' complex argument.

18. Benson, *op. cit.*, p. 50.

19. Bernard C. Rosen, "Social Class and the Child's Perception of the Parent," *Child Development*, 35 (December 1964), 1147–1153.

20. James H. S. Bossard and Eleanor Stoker Boll, *The Sociology of Child Development*, 4th ed. (New York: Harper & Row, 1966), pp. 39–40.

21. Bossard and Boll, *op. cit.*, p. 52. The authors do not identify the source of their census data.

22. Orville G. Brim, Jr., "Family Structure and Sex Role Learning by Children: A Further Analysis of Helen Koch's Data," *Sociometry*, 21 (1958), 1–15.

23. Robert D. Hess and Judith V. Torney, *The Development of Political Attitudes in Children* (Chicago: Aldine, 1967), p. 217.

24. Edmund J. King, *Education and Social Change* (Oxford: Pergamon Press, 1966), p. 3.
25. David A. Goslin, *The School in Contemporary Society* (Glenview, Ill.: Scott, Foresman, 1965), p. 84.
26. Albert J. Reiss, Jr., Introduction to A. J. Reiss, Jr. (ed.), *Schools in a Changing Society* (New York: Free Press, 1965), p. 2.
27. Patricia Cayo Sexton, *Education and Income* (New York: Viking, 1961) reports on one major North American city.
28. S. John Eggleston, *The Social Context of the School* (London: Routledge and Kegan Paul, 1967), p. 26. The quotation describes a study carried out and reported by J. W. B. Douglas, *The Home and the School* (published by MacGibbon and Kee, 1964). American studies reporting comparable practices include W. Lloyd Warner, Robert J. Havighurst, and Martin B. Loeb, *Who Shall Be Educated?* (New York: Harper and Brothers, 1944) and A. B. Hollingshead, *Elmtown's Youth* (New York: Wiley, 1949). Urban population changes in the United States are probably reducing the number of schools in which there is a mixture of social classes, but in smaller cities and towns such mixing probably continues.
29. Robert E. Herriott and Nancy H. St. John, *Social Class and the Urban School: The Impact of Pupil Background on Teachers and Principals* (New York: Wiley, 1966).
30. Herriott and St. John, *ibid.* They found that teacher performance in schools with the lowest-status pupils is judged by principals and fellow teachers to be somewhat less competent than in schools with higher-status pupils.
31. Martin Deutsch, "The Disadvantaged Child and the Learning Process," in Martin Deutsch *et al., The Disadvantaged Child: Studies of the Social Environment and the Learning Process* (New York: Basic Books, 1967).
32. Robert D. Hess, "Effects of Maternal Interaction on Cognitions of Pre-School Children," unpublished paper cited in Norman E. Freeberg and Donald T. Payne, "Parental Influence on Cognitive Development in Early Childhood: A Review," *Child Development*, 38 (March 1967); R. D. Hess and Virginia C. Shipman, "Early Experience and the Socialization of Cognitive Modes in Children," *Child Development*, 36 (1965), 869–886.
33. Fred L. Strodtbeck, "The Hidden Curriculum of the Middle-class Home," in A. Harry Passow *et al.* (eds.), *Education of the Disadvantaged: A Book of Readings* (New York: Holt, Rinehart and Winston, 1967), p. 253.
34. Robert J. Havighurst, "Education and Social Mobility in Four Societies," in A. H. Halsey, Jean Floud, C. Arnold Anderson (eds.), *Education, Economy and Society* (New York: Free Press, 1961), p. 116. For data indicating a similar pattern in Canada, see John Porter, *The Vertical Mosaic* (Toronto: University of Toronto Press, 1965).

35. Natalie Rogoff, "American Public Schools and Equality of Opportunity," in Halsey, *op. cit.*

36. Philip W. Jackson, *Life in Classrooms* (New York: Holt, Rinehart and Winston, 1968), p. 5.

37. *Ibid.*, p. 18.

38. *Ibid.*, p. 20.

39. *Ibid.*, p. 21.

40. Talcott Parsons, "The School Class As a Social System: Some of Its Functions in American Society," *Harvard Educational Review*, 29 (1959), 297–318, reprinted in Talcott Parsons, *Social Structure and Personality* (New York: Free Press, 1964).

41. Robert K. Merton, *loc. cit.*

42. Robert Rosenthal and Lenore Jacobson, *Pygmalion in the Classroom: Teacher Expectation and Pupils' Intellectual Development* (New York: Holt, Rinehart and Winston, 1968), p. vii. This book also includes a summary of other pertinent research on self-fulfilling prophecies.

43. *Ibid.*, p. 70.

44. The evidence relating to the nature of intelligence is analyzed by J. McV. Hunt, *Intelligence and Experience* (New York: Ronald Press, 1961). See also Philip E. Vernon, *Intelligence and Cultural Environment* (London: Methuen, 1969).

45. Eleanor Burke Leacock, *Teaching and Learning in City Schools: A Comparative Study* (New York: Basic Books, 1969).

46. *Ibid.*, p. 205.

47. Iona and Peter Opie, *Children's Games in Street and Playground* (Oxford: Oxford University Press, 1969), p. 17.

48. *Ibid.*, p. 18.

49. Philippe Ariès, "Games, Fashions and Society," in Ariès *et al., The World of Children* (London: Paul Hamlyn, 1966), pp. 101–111.

50. Opie and Opie, *op. cit.*, p. 10.

51. Iona and Peter Opie, *The Lore and Language of Schoolchildren* (Oxford: Oxford University Press, 1959).

52. Ariès, *op. cit.*, p. 107.

53. Opie and Opie, *Children's Games*, p. 3.

54. Harry Stack Sullivan, *The Interpersonal Theory of Psychiatry* (New York: Norton, 1953), p. 245.

55. Carlfred B. Broderick and S. E. Fowler, "New Patterns of Relationships between the Sexes among Pre-adolescents," *Marriage and Family Living*, 23 (February 1961), 27–30.

56. Carlfred B. Broderick, "Sexual Behavior among Preadolescents," *Journal of Social Issues*, 22 (April 1966), 6–21.

57. Boone E. Hammond and Joyce A. Ladner, "Socialization into Sexual Behavior in a Negro Slum Ghetto," in Carlfred B. Broderick and Jessie Bernard (eds.), *The Individual, Sex and Society* (Baltimore: The Johns Hopkins Press, 1969). See also, Carlfred B. Broderick, "Social Heterosexual Development among Urban Negroes and Whites," *Journal of Marriage and Family*, 28 (May 1965), 200–204; Rainwater, *op. cit.*; and Schulz, *op. cit.*

58. Among the general works dealing with mass communications are Charles R. Wright, *Mass Communication: A Sociological Perspective* (New York: Random House, 1959); and Lewis Anthony Dexter and David Manning White (eds.), *People, Society and Mass Communications* (New York: Free Press, 1964).

59. Donald Horton and R. Richard Wohl, "Mass Communication and Para-Social Interaction," *Psychiatry* 19 (August 1956), 215.

60. A study by Melvin L. DeFleur, "Occupational Roles as Portrayed on Television," *Public Opinion Quarterly*, 28 (Spring 1964), 57–74, shows that the occupational roles portrayed on television are disproportionately higher status compared to the distribution of occupations in the actual work world. Television thus does not present children with a realistic array of occupational models. See also Melvin L. DeFleur and Lois B. DeFleur, "The Relative Contribution of Television As a Learning Source for Children's Occupational Knowledge," *American Sociological Review*, 32 (October 1967), 777–789.

61. Anthony Comstock, *Traps for the Young* (Cambridge, Mass.: Belknap Press of Harvard University Press, 1967 reissue, p. 13; original publication: New York: Funk & Wagnalls, 1883).

62. Wilbur Schramm (ed.), *Mass Communications* (Urbana: University of Illinois Press, 1960).

63. Wilbur Schramm and David M. White, "Age, Education and Economic Status As Factors in Newspaper Reading," in Schramm, *op. cit.*, p. 439.

64. Psychiatrist Fredric Wertham some years ago gained wide attention for his view that comic books (as distinct from comic strips in newspapers) have a morally depraving effect on children. See his *Seduction of the Innocent* (New York: Rinehart and Company, 1953).

65. Wilbur Schramm, Jack Lyle, and Edwin B. Parker, *Television in the Lives of Our Children* (Stanford, Cal.: Stanford University Press, 1961), p. 30.

66. Gary A. Steiner, *The People Look at Television* (New York: Knopf, 1963), p. 84.

67. Steiner, *ibid.*, p. 95.

68. Schramm, Lyle, and Parker, *op. cit.*, p. 88.

69. Schramm, Lyle, and Parker, *ibid.*, pp. 96–97. The English study is reported in Hilde Himmelweit, A. N. Oppenheim, and Pamela Vince, *Television and the Child* (London: Oxford University Press, 1958).

70. See, for example, Arnold Arnold, *Violence and Your Child* (Chicago: Henry Regnery, 1969); and Fredric Wertham, *A Sign for Cain: An Exploration of Human Violence* (New York: Macmillan, 1966).

71. Urie Bronfenbrenner, *Two Worlds of Childhood: U.S. and U.S.S.R.* (New York: The Russell Sage Foundation, 1970), p. 114. The concern with violence in the mass media is also reflected in the volume edited by sociologist Otto N. Larson, *Violence and*

the Mass Media (New York: Harper & Row, 1968). This anthology covers movies and printed media as well as TV, although the few empirical studies included deal primarily with TV.

72. Historian Richard Maxwell Brown summarizes the violence that has pervaded the United States since its earliest days. He concludes that "we have always operated with a heavy dependence upon violence in even our highest and most idealistic endeavors." Richard Maxwell Brown, "Historical Patterns of Violence in America," in Hugh Davis Graham and Ted Robert Gurr (eds.), *Violence in America: Historical and Comparative Perspectives* (New York: Bantam Books, 1969), p. 76. See also Richard Hofstadter and Michael Wallace (eds.), *American Violence: A Documentary History* (New York: Knopf, 1970).

73. Eleanor E. Maccoby, "Effects of the Mass Media," in Martin L. Hoffman and Lois Wladis Hoffman (eds.), *Review of Child Development Research*, I (New York: The Russell Sage Foundation, 1964), 323–348.

74. Lotte Bailyn, "Mass Media and Children: A Study of Exposure Habits and Cognitive Effects," *Psychological Monographs*, 73 (1959), No. 1.

75. Maccoby, *op. cit.*, pp. 341–342.

76. Ira O. Glick and Sidney J. Levy, *Living with Television* (Chicago: Aldine, 1962), p. 206.

77. Ralph Garry, "Television's Impact on the Child," in *Children and TV* (Washington: Association for Childhood Education International, 1967), p. 9.

78. Joan Swift, "Effects of Early Group Experience: The Nursery School and Day Nursery," in Hoffman and Hoffman, *op. cit.*, pp. 249–288.

Chapter 6. Conclusion: Socialization in Later Life

1. The dual character of socialization throughout the life cycle was first enunciated in what became a classic paper by anthropologist Ruth Benedict, "Continuities and Discontinuities in Cultural Conditioning," *Psychiatry*, 1 (1938), 161–167, reprinted in Clyde Kluckhohn, Henry A. Murray, and David Schneider, *Personality in Nature, Society and Culture* (New York: Knopf, 1953).

2. George Bernard Shaw's play *Pygmalion*, in which a professor of linguistics teaches a Cockney flower girl to become a "lady," dramatizes an effort to explore the limits of adult socialization. Since the girl had not merely to learn new things for which her previous experience had not prepared her but also had to forget some things she had learned thoroughly, the play is, strictly speaking, about resocialization, the term commonly used to

describe socialization that requires the abandonment of previous socialization.

3. F. Musgrove, *Youth and the Social Order* (Bloomington: Indiana University Press, 1964), p. 33.

4. Beatrice Vulcan, "American Social Policy Toward Youth and Youth Employment," in Melvin Herman, Stanley Sadofsky, and Bernard Rosenberg (eds.), *Work, Youth and Unemployment* (New York: Crowell, 1968), p. 8.

5. Marie Jahoda and Neil Warren, "The Myths of Youth," *Sociology of Education*, 38 (Winter 1965).

6. This trend is discussed by Kenneth Keniston, "Youth: A New Stage of Life," *American Scholar*, 39 (Autumn 1970), 631–654.

7. A more detailed recent summary may be found in Ernest Q. Campbell, "Adolescent Socialization," in David A. Goslin (ed.), *Handbook of Socialization Theory and Research* (Chicago: Rand McNally, 1969), Chapter 20.

8. Talcott Parsons, "Age and Sex in the Social Structure of the United States," *American Sociological Review*, 7 (1942), 604–616, reprinted in Talcott Parsons, *Essays in Sociological Theory*, 2nd ed. (New York: Free Press, 1954).

9. Frederick Elkin and William A. Westley, "The Myth of Adolescent Culture," *American Sociological Review*, 20 (1955), 680–684; and William A. Westley and Frederick Elkin, "The Protective Environment and Adolescent Socialization," *Social Forces*, 35 (1957), 243–249. Parsons himself tempered his views in a later report. See Talcott Parsons, "Youth in the Context of American Society," *Daedalus*, 41 (1962), 97–123.

10. James S. Coleman, *The Adolescent Society: The Social Life of the Teenager and Its Impact on Education* (New York: Free Press, 1961).

11. Bennett M. Berger, "Adolescence and Beyond," *Social Problems*, 10 (1963), 394–408. For two somewhat different studies showing continuity between parental values and adolescent values and conduct see Clay Brittain, "Adolescent Choices and Parent-Peer Cross Pressures," *American Sociological Review*, (June 1963), 385–391; and Richard Flacks, "The Liberated Generation: An Exploration of the Roots of Student Protest," *Journal of Social Issues*, 23 (July 1967), 52–75.

12. Edgar Z. Friedenberg, *Coming of Age in America* (New York: Random House, 1965), p. 42.

13. Edgar Z. Friedenberg, *The Vanishing Adolescent* (New York: Dell Laurel editions, 1962). Berger's article, cited above, compares this volume with Coleman's and with Paul Goodman's *Growing Up Absurd* (New York: Random House, 1960). See also Friedenberg's *Dignity of Youth and Other Atavisms* (Boston: Beacon, 1965).

14. Jahoda and Warren, *op. cit.*, p. 147.

15. Margaret Mead, *Culture and Commitment: Notes on the Genera-*

tion Gap (New York: Natural History Press/Doubleday, 1970).
16. What is now called the generation gap—that is, a presumed large difference in outlook between youth and adults—may actually reflect the rising levels of education and therefore the increased influence on youth of certain types of adults (teachers, writers, professors) and a decreased influence of other types (parents, aunts and uncles, neighbors, police, traditional clergy). Between 1940 and 1970 the proportion of people in the United States with one or more years of college education increased from 13 to 31 percent; college graduates increased from 6 to 16 percent of the young adult population. (Figures from "Census Study Finds an 'Education Gap,'" *The New York Times*, February 4, 1971, p. 1). As the more educated young interact with and differ from the types of adults they knew in childhood, both youth and adult may decide there is a generation gap, overlooking the fact that the young may have simply changed their adult reference groups as they continued their education.
17. The concept of commitment is discussed in Howard S. Becker, "Personal Change in Adult Life," *Sociometry*, 27 (1964), 40–53.
18. Chapter 5, note 60.
19. Herbert Gans's study, *The Levittowners: Ways of Life and Politics in a New Suburban Community* (New York: Vintage Books, 1969), is written as a community study, but many of his observations bear directly on adult socialization.
20. Irving Rosow, "Forms and Functions of Adult Socialization," *Social Forces*, 44 (September 1965), p. 43.
21. Orville G. Brim, Jr., "Socialization through the Life Cycle," in Orville G. Brim, Jr., and Stanton Wheeler, *Socialization After Childhood: Two Essays* (New York: Wiley, 1966), p. 25.
22. Brim, *op. cit.*
23. Stanton Wheeler, "The Structure of Formally Organized Socialization Settings," in Brim and Wheeler, *op. cit.*
24. Charles E. Bidwell, unpublished paper cited by Wheeler, *op. cit.*, p. 70.
25. Howard S. Becker, Blanche Geer, Everett C. Hughes, and Anselm L. Strauss, *Boys in White: Student Culture in Medical School* (Chicago: University of Chicago Press, 1961). See also Fred Davis, "Professional Socialization As Subjective Experience," in Howard S. Becker *et al.* (eds.), *Institutions and the Person* (Chicago: Aldine, 1968).
26. Wilbert E. Moore, "Occupational Socialization," in David A. Goslin (ed.), *Handbook of Socialization Theory and Research* (Chicago: Rand McNally, 1969), Chapter 21. See also Dan C. Lortie, "Shared Ordeal and Induction to Work," in Becker *et al.*, *Institutions and the Person.*
27. Elaine Cumming and William E. Henry, *Growing Old: The Process of Disengagement* (New York: Basic Books, 1961).

28. Matilda White Riley, Anne Foner, Beth Hess, and Marcia L. Toby, "Socialization for the Middle and Later Years," in Goslin, *op. cit.*, p. 952. Italics in original. See also, George L. Maddox, "Retirement As a Social Event in the United States," in B. Neugarten (ed.), *Middle Age and Aging* (Chicago: University of Chicago Press, 1968).
29. An overview of work in this field is given by Reuben Hill and Joan Aldous, "Socialization for Marriage and Parenthood," in Goslin, *op. cit.*, Chapter 22.

Selected Readings

Ariès, Philippe. *Centuries of Childhood*. New York: Random House, 1962.
> The author combines the skills of history, sociology, and art criticism to trace the emergence of the concept of childhood as a distinctive period of the life cycle.

Clausen, John A. (ed.). *Socialization and Society*. Boston: Little, Brown, 1968.
> Eight encyclopedic chapters examine the concept of socialization as used in several disciplines, cross-culturally, and at various phases in the life cycle.

Erikson, Erik H. *Childhood and Society*. New York: Norton, 1950.
> Erikson employs a modified psychoanalytic approach in discussing stages of development and in analyzing the relationship between childhood training and cultural characteristics. These ideas are further developed in the same author's *Identity: Youth and Crisis*, Norton, 1968.

Goldstein, Bernard. *Low Income Youth in Urban Areas: A Critical Review of the Literature*. New York: Holt, Rinehart and Winston, 1967.
> This volume provides both annotated references and integrative summaries of the literature on various aspects of socialization of low-income urban youth.

Goslin, David A. *Handbook of Socialization Theory and Research*. Chicago: Rand McNally, 1969.

This reference work has useful chapters on many aspects of socialization.

Hess, Robert D., and Gerald Handel. *Family Worlds: A Psychosocial Approach to Family Life.* Chicago: University of Chicago Press, 1959.
Five midwestern families of different social class levels are analyzed, using data obtained from the children and parents of each family, to show how the family group functions as a socializing agency.

Hoffman, Lois W., and Martin L. Hoffman. *Review of Child Development Research.* New York: The Russell Sage Foundation, Volume 1, 1964; Volume 2, 1966.
The two volumes are devoted to a summary and overview of some of the main issues in child development.

Jackson, Philip. *Life in Classrooms.* New York: Holt, Rinehart and Winston, 1968.
After observing many elementary school classrooms, the author analyzes some of their main socializing impacts.

Keniston, Kenneth. *Young Radicals: Notes on Committed Youth.* New York: Harcourt Brace Jovanovich, 1968.
The author traces the development from childhood to young adulthood of a group of radicals, showing how personal life histories become intertwined with broader currents of history.

Parsons, Talcott. *Social Structure and Personality.* New York: Free Press, 1964.
These essays by a leading American sociologist examine various aspects of the social structure as they shape socialization.

Piaget, Jean. *The Language and Thought of the Child.* Rev. ed. London: Routledge and Kegan Paul, 1932.
This is one of the earliest and most significant books by this major figure in the study of child development.

Schulz, David A. *Coming Up Black: Patterns of Ghetto Socialization.* Englewood Cliffs, N. J.: Prentice-Hall, 1969.
This intensive study of ten families living in a problem-ridden public-housing project points up some of the special problems besetting black children from low-income families in the course of their socialization.

Sigel, Roberta S. (ed.). *Learning About Politics: A Reader in Political Socialization.* New York: Random House, 1970.
This anthology, devoted to a topic of growing interest, includes papers dealing with many different institutions and processes that influence the development of political beliefs and actions.

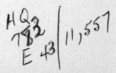

Spiro, Melford E. *Children of the Kibbutz.* Cambridge, Mass.: Harvard University Press, 1958.
    This is a report of a fascinating social experiment. In this Israeli kibbutz, children are reared under a system of collective education; they do not live with their parents and parents have little authority over them.

Strauss, Anselm (ed.). Rev. ed. *George Herbert Mead on Social Psychology.* Chicago: University of Chicago Press, 1964.
    This volume consists of selections from the writings of Mead, noted as the originator of the symbolic interactionist view of self and society.

Vernon, Philip E. *Intelligence and Cultural Environment.* London: Methuen, 1969.
    A noted British psychologist weighs and evaluates diverse evidence to assess the impact of culture on the development of intelligence.

Whiting, Beatrice B. (ed.). *Six Cultures: Studies of Child Rearing.* New York: Wiley, 1963.
    Six teams of anthropologists and associates, each working separately but following the same basic outline, consider the relationships between child training practices and personality differences in communities in Kenya, India, Okinawa, the Philippines, Mexico, and New England.

About the Authors

Frederick Elkin is Professor of Sociology at York University, Toronto, and was Chairman of the Department from 1964 to 1969. Formerly he taught at the University of Montreal, McGill University, and the University of Missouri. He has also been a consultant for Boys Village, in Toronto, and served on the committee that established The Vanier Institute of the Family, in Ottawa.

In addition to having made numerous contributions to the journal literature and to edited works such as *The Unusual Child* (1962) and *The Canadian Family* (1971), Professor Elkin is the author of *Family in Canada* (1964) and a forthcoming book, *Occupations and Ethnic Uprisings: Advertising and Social Change in French Canada.*

Gerald Handel is Associate Professor of Sociology at The City College and Graduate Center of the City University of New York. Formerly he was with the Center for Urban Education; Social Research, Incorporated; and the Committee on Human Development of the University of Chicago. He is Associate Editor of *Journal of Marriage and Family.*

Professor Handel's published work includes *Family Worlds* (1959) and *Workingman's Wife* (1959), of which he is coauthor, *The Psychosocial Interior of the Family* (1967), which he edited, and *The School in the Middle* (1969), of which he is coeditor.